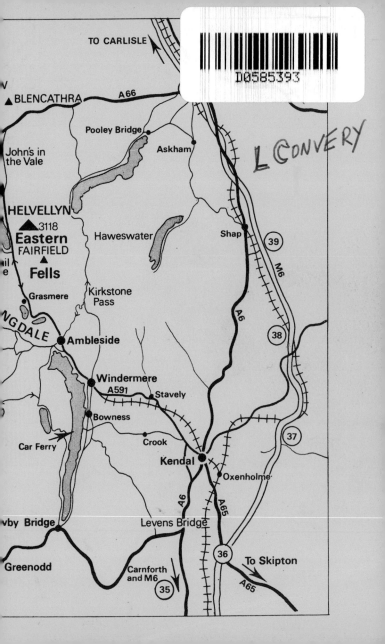

Dublin
Reverse charge

0800 890353

Dub cash call
010 3531

Lakes Weather
from Keswick
0898 - 654691

Rock climbing in the Lake District

This pictorial guide is intended for those wishing to climb in the Lake District in summer or winter

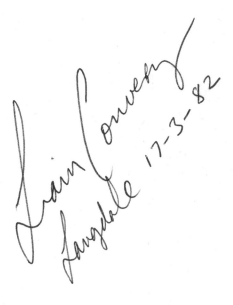

Rock climbing in the Lake District

Geoff Cram
Chris Eilbeck
Ian Roper

An illustrated guide
to selected climbs in
the Lake District

Constable London

First published in Great Britain 1975 by
Constable & Company Ltd
10 Orange Street London WC2H 7EG

Copyright © A. G. Cram, J. C. Eilbeck, I. Roper 1975

2nd edition revised 1977
Reprinted 1981

ISBN 0 09 461840 2
Set in Monophoto Baskerville
Filmset and printed in England at BAS Printers Limited,
Over Wallop, Hampshire

Contents

Maps

Key to maps
●　　　　 = Stretcher Box
M.R.P. = Mountain Rescue Post

Preface to the First Edition

This Guide attempts to describe, with as much pictorial aid as possible, 200 climbs selected from the 1500 climbs currently available in the Lake District. The guide is intended to provide useful coverage for the new visitor to the area or for someone who climbs here only rarely. Nine area centres are given with general information about the local facilities.

The routes are chosen from the direct experience of the three authors over the last fifteen years. We have endeavoured to produce a balanced selection and we hope that there is something for everyone. A novel idea is the inclusion of combined climbs where these are particularly good. As far as the quality of the climbs is concerned, we have tried to indicate this by using a star system, grading each climb according to our own experience and a survey of opinion in the climbing world.

The task of selection has been a difficult one, and we have been forced to omit many excellent climbs. For example, no girdle traverses could be included, because it is so difficult to provide the detailed description required. We have given as much information as possible on winter climbing.

Geoff Cram
Chris Eilbeck
Ian Roper
Keswick 1973

Preface to the Second Edition

This second edition appears with the minimum of alteration. We have not made any changes in the basic format of the guide, but we have tried to correct all our errors, and to provide up-to-date information. We have included one more crag: Neckband Crag on Bowfell. We have also included a few of the large number of very hard new climbs which have appeared recently in the Lake District.

A.G.C., J.C.E., I.R. 1976

Acknowledgements

We are heavily in debt to a great many people for advice, criticism and assistance with both text and photographs. In particular, we are grateful to Peter Lucas for printing many of the photographs.

In addition, we would like to thank Bob Allen, Dave Cook, John Hartley, Bill Lounds and Pete Lucas for photographs, also Jill Aldersley, John Burslem, Jean Cram, Sue Jones, Paul Nunn, Bill Young and some of the above-named for checking the manuscript.

Photographs

R. F. Allen	11, 12, 46, 51, 54, 58, 71, 73, 78
A. G. Cram	2, 3, 49, 79, 81, 86, 88, 90
J. C. Eilbeck	21, 24, 60, 63, 64, 67, 70, 72, 82, 83, 85, 92
C. Hall	65
J. Hartley	61
P. Lucas	19, 22, 23, 48, 91
I. Roper	1, 4–10 inclusive, 13–18 inclusive, 20, 25–45 inclusive, 47, 50, 52, 53, 56, 57, 59, 62, 66, 68, 69, 74–77 inclusive, 80, 84, 87, 89
W. Young	55
K. Wilson	}
I. Roper	} Photographs of the authors

Authors' note

We have endeavoured to check all the information in this book but inevitably some mistakes may have crept in and others will appear as the passage of time changes the details of routes and general information. The authors would be grateful if those readers with corrections or criticisms would send them to Chris Eilbeck, Maths. Dept., Heriot-Watt University, Edinburgh EH14 4AS.

Introduction

The Lake District is one of the most beautiful areas in the country, and offers a fine selection of climbs of all standards of difficulty from the mist-enshrouded bastions of Scafell to the highly popular pitches of Shepherd's Crag. In common with other areas, the climbing population is ever increasing, and queueing for the most popular climbs is now a frequent occurrence. However, to the discerning climber there are always alternatives, and the remote valleys of the Eastern Fells or the combes of Buttermere are frequently empty while the crowds swarm over the Napes or the Langdale crags. One reason for the area's popularity is its accessibility from the great centres of population: Tyneside, South Lancashire, the Midlands and industrial Yorkshire are all now linked to the Lake District by fast roads or motorways, and there is a good rail service to Windermere from the south. Bus services operate through the national park from the south to Keswick, and the Mountain Goat minibus service is expanding rapidly.

For the purposes of this book, the area is divided into geographical sections, usually by valley, in an anticlockwise order starting from Wasdale. Each section also contains general information on the accommodation and other facilities available in the valleys. The crags and climbs are then described in the most convenient or logical order. The terms 'true right' and 'true left' refer to directions facing downstream. Otherwise, right and left are given for the climber facing the crag.

Grading System

We have adopted the generally accepted grading system which has become established over the years, but in an abbreviated form as follows:

E	= Easy	S	= Severe
M	= Moderate	VS	= Very severe
D	= Difficult	HVS	= Hard very severe
VD	= Very difficult	XS	= Extremely severe

Occasionally sub-divisions of these grades are used, e.g. MS = mild severe, HS = hard severe.

Artificial climbs are graded A1 upwards in the conventional way. Where it is possible to grade a winter climb, the Scottish system has been adopted. Note that conditions, and hence grades, are much more variable than in Scotland.

Grade I —straightforward snow climbs with no pitches, though there may be a cornice.

Grade II —gullies with short ice pitches which can be quite difficult. This grade also includes buttresses under winter snow; these should be around very difficult in standard.

Grade III—serious climbs with steep pitches. Buttresses
           around severe in standard.
Grade IV—exacting climbs of the highest standard. Very
           severe buttress climbs.

Star Grading

We have tried to indicate the relative quality of the routes by
giving a star grading: the more stars, the better the route!
While we hope that climbers will find *all* the routes in this
book worthwhile, obviously some climbs are better than
others, and the addition of one, two or three stars
indicates good, very good and outstanding climbs
respectively.

Winter climbing

It is to be emphasised that although good ice conditions are
relatively rare in the Lake District, excellent winter climbs
can often be found. We have given a brief indication at the
end of each section of climbs of which we have experience,
and we have included a description in some cases.
The most reliable areas are still Great End, Gable Crag,
the corries on the east side of Helvellyn and the Scafell
gullies, which provide some of the hardest climbs. It is
essential to ascertain that snow conditions are good as
avalanches are by no means uncommon.

Photographs

Many of the photographs were taken especially for this book.
In fact, in the past year we have had our fingers on the
shutter button more often than on rock! The action pictures
have been taken to give an impression of the style of
climbing on a particular crag or route, while the crag
photographs were intended to yield the maximum amount
of information to aid identification of climbs, and
particularly the starting points and descents.

Maps

Sketch maps covering most of the area described in this
guide are included in each chapter. However, these should
be regarded as merely supplementary to the official
Ordnance Survey 1 inch to the mile Tourist Map of the

Lake District. This is being replaced by the 1:50,000 metric map. Our book is designed to be used in conjunction with the O.S. map, and every crag, mountain rescue point etc. has been pinpointed with the appropriate six-figure grid reference number. We recommend that every party visiting the Lake District should have a copy of this map and know how to use it. The 1:25,000 maps (approx. 2½ inches to one mile) are also most useful.

Other guide books

A comprehensive series of guides is published by the Fell and Rock Climbing Club, and these contain descriptions of all the routes in the area at the date of publication. New routes are collected and published biannually in the FRCC Journal, and in interim guides (paperback).

Information

There are tourist information offices at Ambleside and Keswick, and at the Brotherswater camp site in Patterdale in the summer. Radio Carlisle (206m.) broadcasts regular weather forecasts and tourist information. A Lake District weather forecast is available daily on a 24-hour service, tel. Windermere 5151.

Mountain Safety and Accident Procedure

Mountain safety

Safety precautions appropriate to high mountain areas should always be taken when climbing on the higher crags of the Lake District. Carry waterproofs, spare clothing and food, map, compass, whistle and torch. In winter an ice axe is essential: crampons and ice-climbing gear are necessary if hard snow or ice is to be tackled. In winter or summer, rain combined with lichenous rock can create dangerously slippery conditions and increase gradings, especially on the high north-facing crags such as Pillar or Scafell. For these conditions socks worn over boots or P.A.s are an effective but expensive way of increasing friction.

Route-finding in mist requires skill and experience, and the difficulties of a complicated descent, such as that from Pillar Rock, are enormously magnified by mist, severe weather or darkness. If an unfamiliar descent in these conditions is contemplated, the route should be reconnoitred beforehand, and adequate time should be allowed for both ascent and descent.

Study the map and guide before setting out, and learn the position of mountain rescue posts. Leave word where you are going. If you change your plans and decide not to return, or if you descend into the wrong valley by mistake, inform the police immediately, to prevent the alert of a rescue party.

In winter conditions, avalanche danger should not be underestimated. Gullies, especially those with wide upper slopes or large cornices, are the most prone to avalanches, and should be avoided immediately after heavy snowfall or during a sudden rise in temperature. Central Gully on Great End, for instance, has been the scene of several avalanche accidents.

Buy the Mountain Rescue Committee Handbook (25p) and study the excellent advice and information given there.

Accident procedure

It is important to make the patient as comfortable as possible. Keep him/her warm but do not overheat. Render first aid (see below), and in the case of exhaustion or a minor accident move the victim to shelter. In more serious cases, a shelter of (e.g.) heather, stones or snow blocks should be built round the patient until a stretcher can be brought. If there are more than two in a party, one should stay with the injured man while the others go for help. *It is very important to mark the position of the victim as conspicuously as possible.* If the victim must be left alone he should be tied to the rock to prevent him wandering off in a shocked or semi-conscious state.

Never underestimate the dangers of shock or exhaustion, if you are in any doubt whether to call out the rescue team.

Those going for help should proceed at a speed consistent with safety to the nearest manned Mountain Rescue Post or telephone. They should carry a written message, if possible, stating the location of the victim, the time of the accident, and a description of the injuries sustained. If a telephone is reached first, ring 999 and ask for the Police: they will alert the appropriate Mountain Rescue Team.

First Aid

Keep cool. This helps you and the patient. Reassure the patient. Again, this helps you as well.

Check, in the following order:—
1) breathing and airway   2) bleeding   3) broken bones.

1) Maintaining an airway

1. Clear the mouth and throat of teeth, blood and other debris with a finger and rag; pull the tongue forward.
2. If the airway is still obstructed (noticed by gurgling and rattling), turn the patient gently on to his side with his head downhill and ease his head back fully to straighten his neck and therefore his windpipe.
3. If there is no spontaneous breathing, start mouth-to-mouth artificial respiration and check to see if he has a pulse.
Open the mouth by pressing on the chin. Pinch the nose with your other hand and blow into the mouth. It takes a surprising amount of effort, so check that the chest is rising. If there are severe mouth injuries, blow up the nose.

If there is no pulse, start cardiac massage as well. Kneel by the patient's left side with your hands crossed on the lower breast bone, and lean forward sharply onto straight arms once a second. Every ten strokes, inflate the lungs as above.
4. Check for penetrating chest wounds. Try to make them air-tight with a dressing (e.g. polythene bag and bandage). This is not so urgent as stages 1–3 and should be done after any bleeding has been stopped.

2) Controlling bleeding

Bleeding can be hidden by clothing so check all over. Bleeding even from big blood vessels can almost always be stopped by firm pressure.
Press a hand onto the bleeding point initially (the conscious patient can do this) till replaced by a pad pressed on for about 10 minutes, then bandage the pad firmly. (The pad doesn't have to be fancy: a stone in a handkerchief will do.) Elevate the injured limb.
A tourniquet may be used:—
1) as a temporary measure till direct pressure can be applied
2) as a last resort
3) on complete amputation of limbs.

3) Broken bones

The signs are pain, swelling and deformity. Immobilisation reduces pain and, therefore, shock and further damage. Formal splints will not normally be available, so improvise. Don't bind them too tightly.
Upper arm Bandage to the chest and support the forearm with an improvised sling round the neck.
Forearm Improvise a splint or use the good forearm; arms folded

across the chest. Again, support with a sling around the neck.
Thigh Pull the limb straight and, with padding between the legs to fill out hollows, tie the legs together below the hips, and at the knees and ankles. Keep the good leg straight.
Lower leg Put padding between the limbs and tie them together. Loosen the boot laces but don't remove the boot: the patient won't thank you for trying!
Dislocations and breaks at joints Immobilise in the most comfortable position: don't attempt to straighten the limb.
Spine The patient *MAY* complain of numbness and immobility. Don't move the patient with back pain till the stretcher arrives, then transfer to the stretcher with the back and neck held immobile.

Morphia

The morphia in Mountain Rescue boxes is given by injection into the pinched-up skin. Don't give it to unconscious patients: they don't feel pain. Severe pain worsens shock and will be relieved by morphia. The skin circulation in shocked patients is poor, so massage the injection site. Don't give more than two ampoules in any 2-hour period, or when the skin circulation improves in hospital the drug will all come through in a dangerous rush. For children under 12 years use no more than two ½-ampoules in 2 hours. Note the time of each injection.

General

Arrange some shelter round the patient and some insulation underneath and on top:—e.g. heather, bracken etc. Now you can send for help. Hot sweet drinks are now called for all round.

Never assume a person is dead until first aid measures have been tried for 15 minutes without restoration of spontaneous breathing. These should include artificial respiration and cardiac massage. Any patient who could be suffering from exposure should be presumed alive.

Exposure

A full discussion of this common and dangerous condition is given in the B.M.C. leaflet "Exposure". Stop further heat loss by shelter, dry windproof clothing and snuggling together. Give hot sweet drinks if possible, but not alcohol. Transport the patient on a stretcher, head downhill.
NB If a member of the party is suffering from exposure, then others, including yourself, may be dangerously close to it.

Reference: GARDNER, A. WARD & ROYLANCE, Peter J. (1972): *New Essential First Aid* (Pan Books)

The superb climbing surrounding the valley-head is approached by road from the coastal plain, along the north side of Wastwater. Opposite are the famous screes (no rock climbs—dangerously loose except for some gullies and one small buttress) while on the north side Buckbarrow (136059) and Yewbarrow (170079) offer some short climbs. At the east end of the lake the path winding up Brown Tongue to Scafell and Scafell Pike is clearly visible. The road ends at Wasdale Head: a tiny village overshadowed by some of the highest Lakeland fells. To the north-west lie Mosedale and Pillar Mountain (Pillar Rock is on the opposite side and is described under Ennerdale) while to the north-east is Great Gable with a profusion of buttresses.

The valley is traditionally the finest centre for rock-climbing, with all grades of difficulty on good rhyolite. The routes are generally well-protected and possible in wet weather, while in winter good snow and ice gullies are to be found in the area, particularly on the north face of Great End. It should be noted that routes on Gable Crag can be difficult in bad conditions, but Pike's Crag and the south-west face of Great Gable dry very quickly and face the afternoon sun.

Access

The best approach is by road from Gosforth or Santon Bridge on the coastal plain. Apart from routes along the coast roads, Santon Bridge can be reached from Ambleside over the Wrynose and Hardknott passes. There is a Mountain Goat minibus service on this route twice a day in the summer months. The last petrol station is at Gosforth (9 miles from Wasdale Head) and generally closes at 6 pm.

Rail services from north and south serve Seascale. From here it would be necessary to take a bus to Gosforth or call a taxi (Rigg's in Gosforth, tel. 225, until 4.30 pm weekdays). The only bus service which approaches Wasdale does the return journey Whitehaven—Gosforth—Strands on Thursday morning and evening only (for the market at Whitehaven).

Wasdale Head can be reached on foot from Seathwaite in

1 *Wastwater and Wasdale Head, showing Great Gable in the background.*

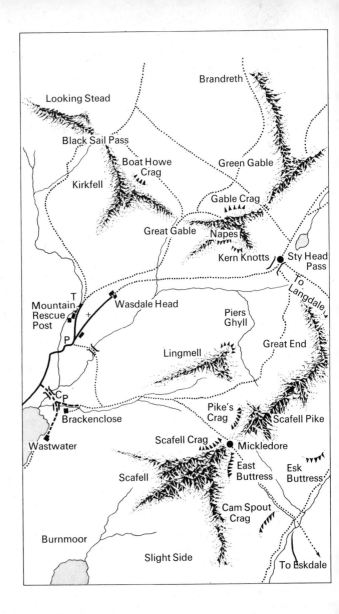

Looking Stead

Black Sail Pass

Boat Howe Crag

Kirkfell

Brandreth

Green Gable

Gable Crag

Great Gable

Napes

Kern Knotts

Sty Head Pass

To Langdale

T

Mountain
Rescue
Post

P

Wasdale Head

Piers
Ghyll

Great End

Lingmell

C P

Brackenclose

Wastwater

Pike's
Crag

Scafell Pike

Scafell Crag

Mickledore

East
Buttress

Esk
Buttress

Scafell

Cam Spout
Crag

Burnmoor

Slight Side

To Eskdale

Borrowdale in 1½ hours, or even from Langdale via
Rossett Ghyll and Esk Hause (about 3 hours).

Accommodation and Camping

At Wasdale Head camping is restricted to the official
National Trust camp site at 183075. A favourite spot for
high camping (for those who can survive the carry up
Brown Tongue!) is Hollow Stones, under Scafell Crag
(206073), where there is also a bivouac boulder. At Wasdale
Head there are the Wastwater Hotel (tel. Wasdale 229) and
several guest houses. Others are found 5 miles away at
Strands. The Youth Hostel, Wasdale Hall, is at the west end
of the lake, 4 miles from Wasdale Head (145045; tel.
Wasdale 222). At Wasdale Head there is a Fell & Rock
Climbing Club hut at Brackenclose (185073), and a
bunkhouse is attached to the Wastwater Hotel. There is an
Achille Ratti Club hut at Buckbarrow (136054).

Food and Drink

At Wasdale Head the hotel and guest houses provide meals.
At the west end of the lake there are hotels and guest houses
in surrounding villages and in adjacent Eskdale.
Milk and other supplies can be bought from the National
Trust camp-site shop and from Wood How Farm, Nether
Wasdale. The nearest shopping centres are Gosforth and
Seascale (early closing day Saturday). Traditional climbers'
drinking is at the Wastwater Hotel: alternatives are the Bridge
Inn at Santon Bridge and the Screes Hotel at Strands. The
local licensing hours are 11–3 pm and 5.30–10.30 pm on
weekdays and 12–2 pm and 7–10.30 pm on Sundays, with
11 pm closing on Fridays and Saturdays.

Garages and Car Hire

The nearest garage is Rigg's at Gosforth, 9 miles from
Wasdale Head. This is the last port of call for petrol, and
closes at 6 pm. There is a motorists' shop, and the garage
does repairs until 4.30 pm on weekdays (tel. Gosforth 225).
The nearest AA garage is Mitchell's at Holmrook (tel. 228,
night 250).

Rigg's Garage provides a taxi service until 4.30 pm on
weekdays (tel. Gosforth 225). Cars can be hired in
Whitehaven: telephone 2697 or 2311.

General Services

Telephones are to be found at the Wastwater Hotel and at

Santon Bridge. There are toilets at the Wastwater Hotel and at the National Trust camp site. There is a good mountaineering supply shop at Westwater Hotel, which also sells guidebooks.

Mountain Rescue
For assistance, ring first the local POLICE, giving as much information as possible. They will contact the Mountain Rescue teams which are based at the Outward Bound Mountain School, Eskdale, and at Keswick and Langdale. Stretchers and first-aid kits are available at the following points:— Mickledore (210069); Styhead Pass (219095); Wastwater Hotel (187088); Eskdale Outward Bound Mountain School (144002) and Seathwaite Farm, Borrowdale (235121).

SCAFELL CRAG (208068)

Four tremendous buttresses containing some of the best climbs in the Lake District rise on the north side of Mickledore. From left to right they are Central Buttress, Pisgah Buttress, Scafell Pinnacle and Deep Ghyll Buttress (standing above the Shamrock). Similarly the three main gullies are Moss Ghyll, Steep Ghyll and Deep Ghyll. The climbs are described from left to right.

Approach: From Wasdale take the well-marked path which starts from the car-park at the head of the lake and continues beside Lingmell Beck. Eventually climb the steep grass of Brown Tongue to the combe below the crags (Hollow Stones)—about 1½ hours. From Borrowdale the easiest route is via Sty Head Pass and the Corridor Route. This leads to the col between Scafell Pike and Lingmell, from which a path contours round below Pikes Crag towards Scafell Crag. Time: 2–2½ hours. From Eskdale follow the approach for Esk Buttress, then go straight up to Mickledore from the waterfall of Cam Spout. Time: 2½–3 hours. Scafell is occasionally approached from Langdale although this is rather a long walk. Ascend Rossett Ghyll and continue to Esk Hause. Follow the tourist path over Scafell Pike to Mickledore. About 3 hours.

Descent: From Central Buttress, down a well-scratched scramble towards Mickledore, the last 60 feet requiring care

2 Central Buttress, Scafell Crag

(Broad Stand; moderate). From the Pinnacle or Deep Ghyll descend the upper part of Deep Ghyll (steep and rather loose) taking care to bear true left into Lord's Rake via the West Wall Traverse (easy).

1 **Botterill's Slab** ** VS
235ft. *F. Botterill, H. Williamson, J. E. Grant 1903*
A tremendous, classic slab climb following the narrow slab on the left of the Central Buttress. Start up a chimney directly below the slab.
1) 50ft. Follow the chimney and rocks above to a good stance and belay. 2) 120ft. Cross onto the slab and follow the face and left edge, in an exhilarating position, to a small niche. Continue directly up the slab to a large ledge and belay. It is possible to traverse right a few feet above the niche to a chimney—either for a runner or an easier alternative to the last part of the slab. 3) 65ft. Easy climbing up the gully at the right.

2 **The Nazgul** * XS
285ft. *L. Brown and K. Jackson 1967*
This fine route takes the thin crack up the left-hand side of the Great Flake of the Central Buttress. Start up a short crack immediately right of Botterill's Slab.
1) 60ft. Climb the crack and easy ledges rightwards to a stance and belay directly below the crack. 2) 85ft. Move up to the crack and climb it using two pitons and a sling for aid. From the second piton climb the very steep wall into a niche and exit from this on its right-hand side, followed by a swing left onto a narrow slab. Follow the slab to a pedestal and continue on good holds to Jeffcoat's Ledge on Central Buttress. A strenuous pitch. 3) 40ft. Climb the wall to the pinnacle on Pitch 6 of Central Buttress and follow the latter to the large ledge and belay. 4) 40ft. Above on the left is a line of narrowing slabs. The first few feet are difficult but the holds improve and a good flat ledge and belay are soon reached. 5) 60ft. Step left onto the dwindling slab and follow this over a bulge until forced onto the steep wall on the left. A final difficult move in a superb situation leads to the top.

3 Botterill's Slab, Scafell Crag

4 Scafell Crag.
R = Rake's Progress. 6 = Moss Ghyll. Route 3 shows the normal start and finish of Central Buttress.

3 **Central Buttress** *** HVS
520ft. *S. W. Herford, G. G. Sansom 1914*
Probably the greatest classic climb in the whole of the
Lake District. The route described actually follows the
Direct Start and Direct Finish, giving a sustained climb
which includes the best pitches of the normal route. Start
where the Rake's Progress path crosses Moss Ghyll at a
corner below a large roof.

1) 65ft. Climb the corner then the rib to a good stance
below an overhanging roof. Peg belay recommended.
2) 75ft. Traverse left for 10ft. to a corner. Climb this and
the wall above, bearing left to the Oval. Belay at the foot
of the Flake Crack.   3) 65ft. Climb diagonally left to gain
the crack and ascend to the large chockstone. From here
either a bold layback or difficult wedging enables good
holds on top of the flake to be reached. Traverse the crest of
the flake to belay.   4) 45ft. Continue along the crest to a
small tower. Shortly after this descend an easy crack to a
large ledge (Jeffcoat's Ledge).   5) 60ft. Follow the ledge
and leftward slanting slab to a block belay.   6) 40ft. Move
down and traverse delicately right along a sloping ledge
past a small pinnacle to a corner. Climb this, then the
outside wall to a large recess. There is a belay at the left
end of the ledge.   7) 90ft. From the left end of the ledge
climb a short slab then follow some ledges to a gangway.
This leads to an overhanging crack with an awkward
finish. Belay.   8) 80ft. Climb the mossy crack in the
corner to easy ground.

4 **Moss Ghyll Grooves** *** MVS
260ft.   *H. M. Kelly, Blanche Eden-Smith, J. B. Kilshaw 1926*
One of the best climbs at this standard in the area, following
an excellent series of grooves to the left (true right) of
Moss Ghyll. Starts in the gully at the top of pitch 3.

1) 55ft. Climb the slanting groove to a good ledge.
Surmount the overhanging block on the right to a grassy
corner and belay.   2) 45ft. Up the corner for a few feet,
then traverse left (crux) onto the edge (the Pedestal). Climb
the arete leading back to the groove and continue to a
stance and belay.   3) 20ft. Climb the narrowing slab until
an easy traverse leads right into the next groove. Large
belay.   4) 80ft. Climb the slab above to a recess. Belay on
the right in a hole or round a block on the slab above.

5) 6oft. Ascend the left wall of the gully and move left onto a large ledge. Climb the steep wall above to the summit ridge.

5 **Slab and Groove Route** * VS

24oft. *R. J. Birkett and L. Muscroft 1948*

A very good route with interesting situations. Start at the foot of a huge slab capped by an overhang, on the left (true right) side of Moss Ghyll.

1) 11oft. An excellent pitch. Climb the groove on the right-hand side of the slab until it is possible to traverse left to a thin crack. Go up this until a step left onto the edge can be made. Climb the edge for a few feet then traverse left to a groove. Climb the groove until level with a recess on the left, then step right and ascend a wall to a corner and block belay (above the overhang which caps the slab). 2) 8oft. Follow the groove to a stance and belay. 3) 5oft. Easy climbing leads to the summit.

6 **Moss Ghyll** *** VD

415ft. *J. N. Collie, G. Hastings and J. W. Robinson 1892*

A splendid and traditional gully climb between the Central and Pisgah Buttresses.

1) 3oft. A chimney with overhanging chockstone. The Rake's Progress path crosses above this pitch. 2) 4oft. Climb the corner on the left. Continue into the very deep chimney. 3) 4oft. Climb the chimney from the back out onto the chockstone. A short chimney follows to ledges and a belay. (Pitches 2 and 3 can be avoided on the right if the chimney is wet.) 4) 5oft. Two short chimneys. 5) 25ft. Easy slabs and a short walk into the gully to a recess below the Tennis Court Wall. 6) 25ft. Climb the short steep wall to the Tennis Court. 7) 25ft. Traverse back into the gully and continue to a large cave. 8) 3oft. From the back of the cave climb on to the 'window sill'. Step down and make a short delicate traverse left (the Collie Step) then climb easy slabs to belay in a recess. 9) 25ft. An easy traverse back into the Amphitheatre. Two finishes are described; first the natural continuation of the gully, second an escape left from the Amphitheatre. 10a) 3oft. Climb over two chockstones to belay on the right wall. 11a)

5 Moving left on the crux of Moss Ghyll Grooves

25ft. Back up the chimney and go through a hole to belay on a boulder.   12a) 40ft. Traverse out a little and climb over two strenuous chockstones.   13a) 35ft. A rather awkward chimney is followed by scrambling to the summit.
10b) 50ft. Climb a rib in the left-hand corner of the Amphitheatre, then a crack to ledges and block belay.
11b) 45ft. Climb a crack above the block, then traverse left to an easy chimney. Continue to ledge and belay.
12b) 30ft. A short corner on the left leads to easy ground.

7 **Pisgah Buttress Direct**   MS
450ft.   *S. W. Herford and F. M. J. McConechy   1911*
A pleasant buttress climb. Starts below the middle of the buttress at a shallow corner.
1) 80ft. Trend left for 40ft., then work right and climb an awkward bulge to a little slab. An easier groove slanting up to the left leads to a ledge and belay.   2) 60ft. Easy ledges on the left, followed by an upward traverse to the right under some loose blocks, then climb a corner to a crevasse.
3) 25ft. The corner on the right. Block belay.   4) 30ft. Traverse a good ledge to the left to a large ledge (the Fives Court) and thread belay.   5) 30ft. The corner crack.
6) 40ft. Continue up the crack, over a bulge to easy slabs. These lead to a large block on the right edge of the buttress.   7) 10ft. A difficult pull-up to a ledge.   8) 50ft. Follow the ridge above, then a groove followed by easier rocks.   9) 40ft. A grassy gully.   10) 85ft. Easy slabs.

8 **Scafell Pinnacle via Slingsby's Chimney**   ***   HD
335ft.   *W. C. Slingsby, G. Hastings, E. Hopkinson, W. P. Haskett-Smith   1888*
A varied and interesting route. Start by scrambling up Steep Ghyll (between Pisgah Buttress and Scafell Pinnacle) for 200ft. Just below a steep pitch a series of ledges on the right mark the start of the route.
1) 45ft. Easy rocks and ledges lead to a terrace.   2) 35ft. Easy slabs lead to a deep crevasse.   3) 20ft. Cross the crevasse and climb a slab to the foot of Slingsby's Chimney.
4) 25ft. Climb the awkward chimney.   5) 45ft. The chimney continues more easily.   6) 55ft. Easy rocks and scrambling to the top of Low Man.   7) 55ft. Ascend the Knife-Edge

6 Slab and Groove, Scafell Crag

Arete to a good stance and belay. 8) 55ft. Easy climbing leads to High Man.

Descent: Can be awkward in wet conditions. Down the left (east) side is an easy trough. Descend this and a short overhanging wall to Jordan Gap (top of Steep Ghyll). Easy rocks leftwards lead onto Pisgah.

9 Jones's Route Direct from Lord's Rake *** S

215ft.   *O. G. Jones and G. T. Walker   1898*

A superb route which gives excellent slab climbing on rough rock. Start on the terrace below the Pinnacle (reached via the preliminary section of Steep Ghyll) on the edge of Deep Ghyll.

1) 25ft. An easy slab leads to some detached blocks.
2) 50ft. Gain the sloping gangway and follow it leftwards. Then ascend steeply for a few feet before traversing left to a niche (the First Nest).   3) 25ft. Climb the wall above going slightly left to the Second Nest.   4) 50ft. Follow the shallow gully for 35ft. then traverse delicately left. A short ascent leads to the Waiting Room. Thread belay 10ft above.
5) 30ft. Climb up into the cave and climb onto the triangular ledge projecting at the top right side (the Mantelshelf). Traverse right along the ledge to the easier crack which leads to a good stance and belay.   6) 35ft. The easy chimney leads to the crevasse on Slingsby's Chimney route.

10 Hopkinson's Cairn Direct * S

165ft.   *S. W. Herford and G. W. Sansom   1912*

A fine open climb, rather more sustained than Jones's Route and with less protection. Starts as for Jones's Route.
1) 100ft. Follow the first three pitches of Jones's Route to the Second Nest.   2) 65ft. Climb the shallow corner on the right, then traverse right across the slab to a flat ledge. Climb the undercut slab above (choice of lines) to a small stance, then continue delicately, working right, to good holds. The large ledge supporting Hopkinson's Cairn is reached by a pull-up. Belays on the ledge are rather poor and it may be preferable to take a stance just below.

From Hopkinson's Cairn, Low Man is reached by the following climb (D, 170ft.). Climb the corner on the left, then step right to a belay. Continue up until the wall on the left can be crossed to another stance. Follow slanting gangways, then an easy chimney and scrambling leads to Low Man.

7 *Scafell Pinnacle*
 SG = Steep Ghyll. DG = Deep Ghyll. WW = West Wall
 Traverse

15

11 Moss Ledge Direct * MVS

335ft. *F. Graham and G. M. Wellburn 1925*

A good slab climb, delicate and serious. The Jones's Arete
Finish from Hopkinson's Cairn is also described. About
halfway along the Pinnacle Terrace it goes over a small
buttress. Start at the foot of this buttress.

1) 40ft. The face of the Buttress leads to the terrace.

2) 30ft. A rib on the wall leads with difficulty to a ledge.
Continue to a niche and belay (the First Nest).   3) 120ft.
Follow a diagonal fault up to the right and round a nose of
rock. Continue up slabs to some sloping ledges which are
climbed at the right-hand end. Traverse left across the top
step to reach Moss Ledge. Continue up Herford's Slab to a
stance and belay either on or just below Hopkinson's Cairn.

4) 70ft. Climb a small groove in the arete between the front
face and the Deep Ghyll wall to a small overhang. Pass this on
the left and follow easier rock tending right to a ledge and
poor belays in the 'Bad Corner'.   5) 20ft. The smooth exposed
slab on the right is climbed from left to right (the Bad Corner).

6) 35ft. Jones's Arete. Follow the crest to belay on a large
block.   7) 20ft. An easy crack leads to the top of Low Man.

12 Woodhead's Climb * MS

160ft *A. G. Woodhead and W. L. Collinson 1907*

A short route with a good finish. Starts at the corner where
the Deep Ghyll Wall of the Pinnacle meets the wall which
runs down from Professor's Chimney. (The deep-cut
chimney descending from Jordan Gap.)

1) 30ft. Get on to a slab on the Deep Ghyll Wall, move
left and climb directly to a good ledge and belay.   2) 55ft.
From the left end of the ledge, climb the wall above and
work right to follow the arete to a large recess. Belay.

3) 45ft. Herford's Finish. Gain a corner on the left, then
cross the slab above rightwards to a small ledge. Go straight
up over a bulge then step left. Up to a stance and belay.

4) 30ft. An awkward step is followed by easy rocks to High Man.

13 West Wall Climb D

185ft. *J. W. Robinson, T. H. Doncaster and H. W. Blunt 1890*

A pleasant route with short pitches. The start is 50ft to the
right of the Great Chimney (VD), a prominent landmark
on the Deep Ghyll side of Deep Ghyll Buttress.

1) 30ft. A deep chimney.   2) 25ft. An awkward corner
leads to a ledge.   3) 25ft. The chimney on the left.

4) 35ft. Climb the wide corner ahead, starting on the left and finishing to the right.   5) 10ft. Easy rocks to the foot of an arete.   6) 40ft. Climb the arete.   7) 20ft. A little chimney, then a small cave pitch leads to the top.

SCAFELL EAST BUTTRESS   (210068)

This magnificent barrel-shaped crag stretches for almost ¼ mile in a south-easterly direction from Mickledore. It provides a network of high standard routes on superb rock, and this, coupled with the magnificent outlook, makes its climbs among the finest in Lakeland. Unfortunately the cliff is frequently wet, since it takes a considerable amount of drainage, and the rock becomes abominably greasy in a very short time. As a result, the climbs are serious for their length and standard, and parties attempting any of the climbs on this crag should be capable of organising a safe escape for themselves in the event of failure or bad weather. The climbs are described from right to left, the order in which they are approached from Mickledore, the usual base for operations in the area.

Approach: See Scafell Crag.

Descent: At the top right-hand side of the crag a short gully leads down into Mickledore chimney. Cross this to join the scrambling route down Broad Stand onto Mickledore (with a short stretch of climbing at moderate standard).

14   **Chartreuse**   *   HVS
190ft.   *R. Smith and D. Leaver   1958*
A facet of the buttress rising out of Mickledore chimney yields the first climb. Start by scrambling up Mickledore chimney until it is possible to break back left to a ledge and poor belay below the large slab.
1) 70ft. Traverse delicately left until it is possible to follow a shallow corner up the edge of the slab to a stance and belay in a corner on the left. A poorly protected pitch.
2) 90ft. Climb the corner above to the overhang and move right onto the slab. Continue up the crack to a large overhang and traverse right to a very steep fist-wide crack. Follow this with difficulty to a large stance.   3) 30ft. A short crack and easy rocks lead to the top.

15 **Fulcrum** ** VS
18oft.   *K. Jackson and J. Adams 1968*
A good climb which winds its way through an impressive
part of the crag. Start up the chimney directly below the
twin grooves of Mickledore Grooves (q.v.).
1) 5oft. Climb the chimney and the right-hand groove to a
small stance and belay.   2) 6oft. Step down and left onto
the steep wall. Climb this then traverse left under an
overhang to enter the base of a groove. Climb up the
groove to the stance at the top of pitch 2 of Leverage.
3) 7oft. Continue up the groove to the overhang, then take
the steep left-hand crack. Pull out right at the top, move
leftwards to an arete, then continue to the top.

16 **Leverage** * XS
18oft.   *R. Smith and D. Leaver 1958*
The crack line which splits the first pitch of Mickledore
Grooves gives a strenuous climb.
1) 25ft. The impending crack 15ft. right of Mickledore
Grooves is climbed onto the slab. Follow this up to the
right to a ledge and belay.   2) 75ft. Move back left into
the crack and follow this over three bulges into a groove
which leads more easily to a small ledge and belay on a rib.
Move right into a corner to a better stance and belay.
3) 8oft. Follow the corner to a small overhang. Pull round
this to the right to gain a slab, and follow this to the top.

17 **Mickledore Grooves** *** VS
225ft.   *C. F. Kirkus, I. M. Waller and M. Pallis 1931*
Notable for its long final pitch. Start 25yds. left of Mickledore
chimney, where a short slab slants up to the right.
1) 85ft. Pull onto the slab and follow it up to the right to
the foot of a pair of grooves. Climb the left-hand groove,
and after 15ft. transfer into the right hand groove. Follow
this to a ledge and belay in a big corner.   2) 14oft. Step
round to the right onto a large slab and after a step up to
the left a diagonal crack can be followed rightwards into a
big groove. Climb the groove until the angle eases and a
ledge can be reached on the right. Follow the ledge round
the corner until a short awkward wall can be climbed to
the top.

8 Scafell East Buttress, Right Flank

9 Scafell East Buttress, Left Flank

18   **May Day Climb**   **   HVS

270ft.   *R. J. Birkett, C. W. Hudson and C. R. Wilson   1938*
G. Oliver and L. Willis   1959

A strenuous climb, frequently wet, which takes the big
slanting groove in the upper part of the crag, some 30ft.
left of Mickledore Grooves. Start at a narrow slab inset in
the impending wall some 12 yards left of Mickledore
Grooves.

1) 60ft. Climb the slab (more strenuous than it appears)
until a traverse right leads to a small stance and piton belay
below a small steep groove.   2) 50ft. Climb the groove with
difficulty until the angle eases and the big groove can be
entered. A sloping ledge and thread belay are reached on
the left.   3) 80ft. Continue up the crack above the belay
and follow the corner on the right, using a crack in the
right wall, to a piton. Move right above the piton to gain
the arete and follow this to a stance above the corner.
4) 80ft. The wide crack and easy slabs lead to the top.

19   **Overhanging Wall**   *   VS

205ft.   *M. Linnell and A. T. Hargreaves   1933*

A route of some delicacy despite its steepness. Start below and
left of May Day Climb on an overhung ledge.

1) 85ft. Move up to the left to a good ledge, then ascend a
little before traversing right and up to gain a 'saddle'.
Step down to the right and climb a crack using a piton to
a resting place. Step right again and climb steeply on small
but good holds until a grass ledge in a corner is reached.
2) 120ft. Traverse left and down onto the White Slab and
climb it to a large square block. Continue up the Slab
until it is possible to work into a mossy corner on the right
(often wet). Break back left and continue into the final
gully. Belay. Scrambling leads to the top.

20   **Centaur**   ***   HVS

320ft.   *L. Brown and S. Read   1960*

Sustained, exposed and varied climbing combined with
difficult route-finding make this one of the finest routes on
the East Buttress. Start 20ft. right of the lowest point of
the crag.

1) 60ft. Climb the groove on good holds, passing a large
ledge to a corner stance and piton belay.   2) 50ft. 15ft.
above the ledge, on the left edge of the corner, is a small

resting place. Gain this, starting from the corner; go up then traverse back right, across the groove, to a comfortable ledge and peg belay. 3) 50ft. Traverse right into a shallow corner parallel to the main groove and climb this for 15ft., then traverse back left along a sloping shelf to regain the main corner and follow this to a slab stance. Piton belay. 4) 60ft. Above is an impending wall in which is inset a thin horizontal slab. Gain this from a point about 15ft. to the right, then traverse the slab left to a scoop (often wet, good thread runner). Climb the scoop, with an awkward finish, onto a slab, and up this to a piton belay. 5) 30ft. Climb a crack on the left to a precariously perched pinnacle. Stance and belay on the far side of the pinnacle. 6) 70ft. Leave the ledge on the left then trend back right at once and go up the steep wall to a corner of blocks. Climb the magnificent layback crack above—a spectacular finish!

21 **Great Eastern Route** *** MVS
225ft. *M. Linnell and S. H. Cross, 1932*
A magnificent climb with no great difficulties. Start by scrambling up an opening 20ft. right of the lowest point of the crag and walking left to an overhung ledge.
1) 70ft. Follow a gangway up to the left to an overhang. Continue up the crack on good holds to a hanging slab on the left. Cross the slab, pull up the corner and traverse left to an exposed rib which is climbed to a good stance and belay. 2) 30ft. Climb the twin cracks above to a stance and belay below a roof. 3) 75ft. Traverse the slab on the right, then go up a step before continuing the traverse to a small crevasse. 4) 30ft. Move up a corner then either climb a chimney on the right or the wall on the left. 5) 20ft. Go up and round the corner on the right to a ledge at the top of the White Slab. Belay in the corner.

21A **The Yellow Slab** *** HVS
175ft. *M. Linnell and H. Pearson 1933*
This variation finish, which has very fine situations indeed, starts from the top of pitch 1 of Great Eastern Route.
2) 110ft. A pinnacle on the left is used as a starting point for this pitch. Step off the pinnacle and up a short crack (often wet) to the foot of the Yellow Slab. Climb the centre of this to the foot of a steep wall, when a move left brings one to the foot of a jamming crack. Climb this to a small

stance and belay on the left in a superb situation.   3) 60ft.
Move left along the ledge and pull up the corner with the
aid of some large, if dubious, flakes. Continue traversing
left on sloping holds until a final awkward move gives
access to the top of the crag.

22   **Gold Rush**   *   XS
410ft.   *A. G. Cram and W. Young   1969*
This route starts along the terrace, about 40ft. left of Great
Eastern Route below a wet corner.
1) 130ft. Pull over the steep walls on the right then traverse
left to the corner. Climb through the water to the overhang,
which is climbed on improving holds. Continue up the
slab and two short walls to the stance and pinnacle belay of
Great Eastern.   2) 50ft. Follow easy ledges horizontally
left, then climb a black wall and traverse a short slab to a
poor stance and peg belay below a long corner.   3) 50ft.
Climb the corner and crack direct to the top of the Yellow
Slab. Stance and chockstone belays.   4) 100ft. Continue
up the crack to the big overhang. Move out left then
continue up the wall and slab above to a large ledge and
peg belay.   5) 80ft. Easy rocks to the top of the crag.

23   **Ichabod**   ***   XS
310ft.   *G. Oliver, G. Arkless and N. Brown   1960*
The large rightward facing corner on the left of Great
Eastern Route gives the line of this magnificent climb.
Below the corner is a leftward slanting gangway which
provides the first pitch.
1) 50ft. The gangway is followed to an overhung stance.
2) 80ft. Pull round the overhang to the right into the
corner. Climb this to a good thread then descend slightly
and traverse right, passing an insecure piton, into a groove,
which is followed until it is possible to pull out to the
right. Either climb directly into the groove above, or,
harder, traverse right and up on sloping holds until a
traverse line runs back left into the groove. Good thread
belay.   3) 110ft. Climb the V-groove on small holds to a
bulge. Move left with difficulty into the main corner and
climb this without further incident to the foot of a final
steep crack which leads to a large platform.   4) 70ft. The
easy buttress on the left leads pleasantly to the top, or walk
off to the left.

24 **Phoenix** ** XS

290ft.   *R. Moseley   1957*

A strenuous sister route to Ichabod. The route takes the line of cracks on the left of the great prow which bounds the corner of Ichabod on the left.

1) 60ft. The easy gangway of Ichabod.   2) 90ft. Climb a crack on the left of the overhang above the stance to a resting place. A finger-jamming crack is followed to a piton on the left, when a shallow chimney just to the right leads to a hard finish onto a rounded ledge. Step left into a groove and follow this on better holds to a grass stance. A sustained pitch.   3) 70ft. Step right and climb the wall by a series of difficult layback moves to good holds at 20ft. Continue straight up until a traverse right can be made to the arete. Follow the arete to the large ledge at the top of Ichabod.   4) 70ft. The buttress above gives pleasant climbing to the top.

25 **Hell's Groove** *** HVS

265ft.   *A. R. Dolphin and P. J. Greenwood   1952*

80ft. left of Ichabod is a big groove guarded by a short impending crack. This sustained climb is one of the best on the East Buttress. Start directly below the crack.

1) 30ft. Climb an easy slab to a stance and belay.   2) 25ft. The crack gives a short but extremely strenuous struggle before the ledge below the main groove can be gained.
3) 80ft. From a small ledge above the stance step into a crack in the right wall and follow this over a series of bulges to a ledge below a steep wall. Climb to a crack above a small block at the right hand end of the ledge and gain the stance above by a final difficult move.   4) 85ft. Climb a crack on good holds to the right of the overhang above, then trend left into an open chimney. Follow the chimney and crack above into an amphitheatre.   5) 45ft. Move up to the left along a crevasse then move back to the right along another crevassed block when a cave pitch leads to the top.

26 **Trinity** * HVS

225ft.   *D. D. Whillans and J. R. Sutherland   1955*

The groove parallel to Hell's Groove yields a climb of

10 *Hard climbing on Ichabod, Scafell East Buttress*

considerable character. Start directly below the groove.

1) 100ft. A short wall leads into the groove which is followed past an awkward overhang to a stance and belay.

2) 95ft. Continue up the open corner over two bulges, the second being passed by a difficult layback. The angle relents and good holds lead up to a rock ledge in a recess. Pull up the short wall on the right to a big grassy ledge.

3) 30ft. The corner and crack above are followed on good holds to the top of the crag.

PIKES CRAG (210072)

Pikes Crag is the large but rather broken crag which faces Scafell across Hollow Stones. The main crag is divided by a ridge which falls from the highest point. This is the line of Grooved Arete. The crag faces south-west and dries quickly, but the climbing in general is not of the same quality as that on Scafell.

Approach: As for Scafell Crag.

Descent: The descent starts from the col joining the crag to the Pike. Descend to the col by a steep crack on good holds, or a broken chimney-groove on the right. Care is needed in wet conditions. Continue down the gully on the Mickledore side (south) of the crag, making a detour on the left to avoid a short pitch.

27 **Grooved Arete** * VD

370ft. *C. F. Holland and G. R. Speaker 1924*

A good climb with much variety, providing a worthwhile expedition in all weather conditions. Starts below the V-shaped hollow capped by an overhang which is a prominent feature of the bottom of the ridge.

1) 60ft. Take the easiest line to the foot of the crack forming the left edge of the overhanging wall above.

2) 40ft. Climb the crack until a traverse left can be made to the edge. Climb this to a large ledge. Belay at the back in a chimney.   3) 70ft. Climb the chimney and continue in the same line to reach an angular corner.   4) 55ft. The crack in the corner is polished and hard to start. After reaching a ledge, traverse left a little, then go up past some blocks and traverse right to a prominent block on the edge of the ridge. (A pleasant alternative to pitches 3 and 4 is to follow the crest of the ridge. This gives open delicate

11 Pikes Crag, from Hollow Stones

26

climbing at severe standard.)   5) 60ft. Ascend the slab
above, work left and then back right to ledges on the
crest.   6) 25ft. Cross the corner on the left and continue up
a slab to a ledge below a huge block.   7) 15ft. Climb the
chimney on the left of the block. A way off can be made
here, but this would miss one of the best pitches.   8) 45ft.
Traverse down the ledge to the left to gain the front of the
ridge. Climb the slab above, with difficulty (especially when
wet) to the summit of the crag.

28 **Sentinel**   *   VS
240ft.   *P. Fearnehough and J. Wright   1960*
A fine climb following the impressive crack up the centre of
the large square-cut pillar about 200ft. left of the rib of
Grooved Arete. Start by scrambling up ledges diagonally
left to the foot of the pillar.
1) 50ft. Climb a shallow crack in the centre of the pillar to
a good ledge and belay directly below the impressive crack.
2) 70ft. Move up and climb the steep crack. Avoid some
doubtful blocks on the right and continue up the crack on
good jams to a ledge and belay.   3) 60ft. Easier climbing to
a ledge and belay below and left of an obvious overhanging
crack.   4) 60ft. Climb the groove to the overhang. Pull
over this (strenuous) and continue up the easier groove to
the top of the crag.

29 **Juniper Buttress**   **   VD
260ft.   *H. M. Kelly and party   1924*
A good route which starts at a large block some 20yds.
right of the left bounding rib of Pulpit Rock.
1) 35ft. Gain a small ledge then traverse right to a corner
crack. Climb this to a stance and belay on the left.   2) 25ft.
A gangway up the wall to the right to a ledge.   3) 35ft.
Surmount a series of blocks finishing up a crack.   4) 50ft.
Scramble up working right to blocks on the edge of a grassy
gully.   5) 55ft. Climb the groove above on the left
followed by a short crack.   6) 60ft. Start at a rib on the
right and climb the exposed wall above using a thin crack.
Easier rocks lead to the top of Pulpit Rock.

30 **Wall and Crack Climb**   **   VD
270ft.   *H. M. Kelly and party   1924*
A pleasant climb which takes the left hand edge of Pulpit Rock.

12 Grooved Arete on Pikes Crag

1) 65ft. Step round to the left of the ridge and climb to a belay. Continue up a steep wall to another stance. 2) 50ft. Climb a vertical crack to a rock platform. A staircase of rock on the right leads to a terrace. 3) 70ft. The wall above is climbed slanting right, followed by a crack in three sections. 4) 35ft. Another rock staircase leads to a ledge. Belay below a crack on the right. 5) 50ft. Climb the steep crack or the wall on its left. Scrambling follows to the top.

KERN KNOTTS (216094)

This short but steep crag lies on the south-west slope of Great Gable and overlooks the Sty Head Pass. The rock is excellent and the routes, though short, have much character, with the advantage that the crag dries very quickly. The Sty Head Face is split by Kern Knotts Crack and Innominate Crack, while the south face is divided by the deep feature of Kern Knotts Chimney.

Approach: From Wasdale ascend Sty Head Pass then take the Gable Traverse path which contours round the south-west face of the mountain. Kern Knotts is reached in 5 minutes from the top of the Pass (about ¾ hour from Wasdale Head). From Borrowdale ascend Sty Head Pass and join the Gable Traverse. Time about 1 hour.

Descent: The best descent from the crag is found on the west side.

31 **The Cenotaph**   VS
120ft.   *P. Ross, R. Scott and D. Wildridge   1955*
A bold but well protected crux. Starts just right of the right-hand corner of the Sty Head face of the crag.
1) 35ft. Climb the chimney to a pinnacle beneath overhangs.
2) 85ft. Climb the steep crack to the roof. Turn this by a swing to the right into a groove which is followed on small holds to the top.

32 **Innominate Crack**   MVS
60ft.   *G. S. Bower, Bentley Beetham and J. B. Wilson   1921*
A much-photographed classic, sustained but not serious with

13 *The 'outside' route on Kern Knotts Crack*

modern protection. Takes the thinner, right-hand of the two cracks splitting the Sty Head Face of the crag.
1) 60ft. Climb the crack, some use being made of a subsidiary crack on the left in the middle third of the pitch.

33 **Kern Knotts Crack**   MVS
70ft.   *O. G. Jones and H. C. Bowen   1897*
A well-polished classic which repulses many would-be tigers. Takes the wide, left hand crack splitting the Sty Head face of the crag.
1) 70ft. Climb the crack to the sentry box. From here climb either the polished crack (strenuous) or the right wall (delicate) to reach the upper part of the crack. The rest of the crack is followed with less difficulty.

34 **Buttonhook Route**   HVS
100ft.   *F. G. Balcombe and C. J. A. Cooper   1934*
A remarkable climb for its time; it is short but strenuous and serious. Start 15ft. left of the corner where the Sty Head and Wasdale faces of the crag meet.
1) 75ft. Climb a pair of twin cracks to the overhang and by means of a long reach gain a wedged flake on the right. Pull over the overhang and continue up a thin crack to a small stance. Traverse horizontally left with increasing difficulty passing a thread runner to an open scoop: climb this on poor sloping holds to a ledge and belay on the right.
2) 25ft. Finish up the rib above.

35 **Kern Knotts Chimney**   *   D
190ft.   *O. G. Jones, W. H. Fowler and J. W. Robinson   1893*
An old-fashioned chimney climb, best attempted without rucksacks. Starts below the deep chimney in the Wasdale face.
1) 70ft. Ascend an easy staircase, then climb the chimney past a chockstone to the top.   2) 50ft. Go under the bridged block to a belay, then up a polished slab.   3) 70ft. Easy slabs lead to the top of the crag.

THE NAPES   (211099)
Following the Gable Traverse from Sty Head, the first obvious feature is the huge expanse of Tophet Wall. The classic Severe on this face takes an impressive slanting line

from left to right between overhangs. Further along the traverse the Needle can be seen, and a higher traverse at this level can be reached by scrambling up on either side of the Needle. 200ft. past the Needle is the Eagle's Nest Ridge, and further round is Abbey Buttress. The next big ridge along the traverse is Arrowhead Ridge. Further on, the prominent landmark of the Sphinx Rock provides an amusing problem.

Descent: By the scree slopes bounding the Napes on either side; Little Hell Gate to the west of the Sphinx Rock and Great Hell Gate to the right of Tophet Wall. The gullies between the Napes ridges are loose and wet and are not recommended in either direction except in good winter conditions.

36 **Tophet Wall** *** S
265ft. *H. M. Kelly and R. E. W. Pritchard 1923*
A superb climb, serious and sustained with the most exciting moves at the end. Starts just left of the middle of the wall and slants to the right.
1) 40ft. Climb up on the right of an overhanging crack, then step into the crack and follow it to a ledge. 2) 45ft. Traverse up to the right to a grass ledge below a wall. This point can also be reached from the ground by an easy traverse from the right. 3) 30ft. The wall is climbed on small holds to a ledge. Move left to a corner. 4) 25ft. Climb the crack in the corner, then ascend the right wall to a corner and belay on the right. 5) 50ft. Traverse right on good handholds to a corner. Climb the rib on the right to a stance. 6) 30ft. Climb a small pinnacle then move back left and follow the steep crack on good jams to a ledge. 7) 45ft. Easier climbing leads to the top.
A short distance further on is an easy gully on the right for the descent.

37 **Tophet Grooves** ** HVS
225ft. *R. J. Birkett and V. Veevers 1940*
The route follows the big groove up the left edge of the Tophet Wall. Start directly below the main groove up a

14 Overleaf left: Tophet Wall, Great Gable

15 Overleaf right: On Tophet Wall, Great Gable

smaller one.

1) 55ft. The groove is awkward to start and leads to a juniper ledge and belay, below the main groove. 2) 50ft. Climb the open groove to the overhang (care needed with a doubtful block) then traverse right across a mossy scoop before climbing up to a belay in the groove on the left.

3) 70ft. Step right and climb a mossy wall to a good ledge. Then follow a grassy crack on the right to a large belay.

4) 50ft. Climb the crack above to the top.

38 **The Needle**   **   HVD
W. P. Haskett-Smith (solo) 1886

This famous pinnacle gives an interesting and nowadays very polished climb with some exciting moves. The following pitches all lead to the Shoulder beneath the top block.

1a) 40ft. The crack splitting the Wasdale face provides a safe but strenuous struggle: easier in descent (if you don't get stuck!). 1b) 50ft. From the foot of the Wasdale crack traverse right to the arete and climb this direct. 1c) 60ft. Climb the crack on the side facing Lingmell. 2) 15ft. From the Shoulder, mantelshelf with difficulty onto the polished ledge on the right-hand edge of the top block. Toe-traverse to the left, then an awkward step up leads to the top. A belay can be arranged by looping the rope round the overhangs of the top block. The descent is not quite as difficult as the ascent, and the last man can be protected by running the rope over the top block.

39 **Needle Ridge**   **   D
325ft. *W. P. Haskett-Smith (solo) 1884*

A justifiably popular climb up the ridge behind the Needle. Starts from the gap behind the Needle. The first pitch is much the hardest on the climb.

1) 35ft. Climb a polished slab to a chimney trending left to a stance. 2) 50ft. A short but steep wall leads to easier rocks. Climb a broken wall to a stance, then walk 25ft. to the rib. 3) 24oft. Follow the scratched and

16 Opposite: Napes Needle

17 Overleaf left: Heavy traffic on Needle Ridge, Great Gable

18 Overleaf right: Eagle's Nest Ridge Direct, Great Gable

obvious route up the ribs and corners; frequent belays.

40 **Crocodile Crack**   HVS
185ft.   *G. Oliver, G. Arkless, P. Ross and N. Brown   1960*
All the interest is concentrated into one long pitch.
Start from the Dress Circle (the large ledge overlooking the
Needle) about 15ft. to the right of Eagle's Nest Direct.
1) 140ft. Climb a flake crack for 25ft. before moving left
onto a steep wall. Climb this and the crack above to an
overhang at 50ft, which is surmounted facing left.
Continue up the crack with good situations to a large
ledge.   2) 45ft. Grassy chimneys lead up to the ridge.

41 **Eagle's Nest Ridge Direct**   **   MVS
120ft.   *G. A. Solly and party   1892*
A sustained and delicate pitch with little protection. Takes
the arete at the left edge of the face overlooking the Needle.
1) 50ft. Climb up steep rock, trending right, to a ledge.
2) 70ft. Traverse left to the edge, using two parallel cracks.
Climb the edge to a small platform (the Eagle's Nest). A
second platform (the Crow's Nest) is reached after a further
15ft. A slab with sloping holds is climbed to reach easy
ground on the ordinary route.

42 **Eagle's Nest Ridge via The West Chimney**   **   HD
355ft.   *G. A. Solly and M. Schintz   1892*
A popular climb and justly so. Start up the battered
chimney on the left of Eagle's Nest Ridge.
1) 70ft. (Can be split.) Easy scrambling and then good
holds in the chimney lead to a large platform.   2) 25ft.
Continue up the chimney with more difficulty to a crevasse.
3) 40ft. Traverse right through the crevasse to a polished
slab which leads with some difficulty to a rock ledge in a
corner.   4) 40ft. The strenuous chimney is climbed onto a
slab. Continue up this to a level crest.   5) 60ft. The
chimney on the left or any one of several well-scratched
variations lead to the next crest.   6) 120ft. Continue up the
crest. Difficulties can be chosen or avoided at will. Stances
and belays at frequent intervals.

43 **Abbey Buttress**   **   VD
180ft.   *F. Botterill and J. de V. Hazard   1909*
A good buttress climb. Starts from the crevasse which is an

obvious landmark on the traverse along the foot of the Napes, about 150ft. left of Eagle's Nest Ridge.

1) 60ft. Climb to a ledge, then step right and ascend a steep crack to a ledge and belay. 2) 65ft. Go up steep rock for 15ft. to a wide ledge. Traverse left for 15ft., then go straight up for 25ft. Traverse right below an overhang, then climb the arete on good holds to a large ledge.

3) 30ft. Climb a crack on the left corner of the buttress.

4) 25ft. Continue up the left edge to join Eagle's Nest Ordinary Route.

44 **Arrowhead Ridge Direct**   *   VD
235ft   *W. C. Slingsby and party 1892*
G. A. Solly and party 1893

One of the best of the Napes ridges. Takes the obvious ridge on the left of the Napes with an unmistakable arrowhead-shaped pinnacle near the top. Starts at the bottom of the ridge.

1) 80ft. Follow the ridge for two pitches. 2) 40ft. Ascend the slab to the base of the Arrowhead which is climbed on good holds. Belay round the top of the Arrowhead.

3) 35ft. Cross the gap and follow the horizontal section of the ridge to a slabby face which leads to a belay. 4) 80ft. Scrambling along the easy upper part of the ridge.

GABLE CRAG   (213105)
Situated on the north face of Great Gable and overlooking Ennerdale, the crag offers excellent climbing after several days of dry weather. In poor conditions, however, the rocks can be exceedingly greasy. The main interest is concentrated on two buttresses: the wall called Engineer's Slabs (!) which lies just right of the centre of the face below the summit, and Mallory's Buttress which lies on the left side of the face and right of a wide scree gully.

Approach: From Wasdale leave the Sty Head path just beyond the bridge and follow a path up the steep south-west ridge of Great Gable (Gavel Neese). Then continue diagonally left to gain the col between Kirk Fell and Great Gable (Beckhead) from which a faint path contours round below Gable Crag. Time—about 1½ hours. From Borrowdale (the easiest approach) it is best to start at the top of Honister Pass. Follow the footpath towards Green Gable

then traverse the Ennerdale flank of the mountain via the
Moses Trod path to a point below Gable Crag. About
1 hour. A longer alternative from Borrowdale would be to
ascend Sty Head Pass and then cross Windy Gap between
the two Gables. The Crag can be reached easily from
Ennerdale, and from Buttermere by first ascending Honister
Pass then following the route above.
Descent: A descent from Engineer's Slabs is described after
the route. From the Slant descend towards Windy Gap.

45 **Sledgate Ridge**   HS
240ft.   *J. Wilkinson, A. H. Greenbank and A. E. Wormell   1958*
An excellent approach to Engineer's Slabs. This route
quickly becomes VS in poor conditions. Start from the
path below and to the left of Engineer's Slabs.
1) 70ft. A difficult crack is followed by a water-worn
groove on the right. After 30ft. ascend a wall on the left
to a large ledge.   2) 60ft. From the left-hand end of the
ledge get onto the wall above and traverse rightwards
across the slabs (little protection) to a large grass ledge.
3) 110ft. The wall above is climbed to the centre one of three
cracks. Follow this to the top. (Descend on the right to reach
Engineer's Slabs).

46 **Engineer's Slabs**   ***   VS
180ft.   *F. G. Balcombe, J. A. Shepherd and C. J. A. Cooper*
1934
A magnificent climb, steep and sustained but much harder in
poor conditions. Starts below the middle of the wall which
is reached by a steep scramble from the foot of the face,
or via Sledgate Ridge.
1) 80ft. Climb a wall on small holds, just left of a short
groove, to a ledge at the top of the groove. Continue up a
crack, then reach a pair of steep cracks which lead to an
obvious chimney. A few feet higher is a sentry box and nut
belay.   2) 55ft. Traverse right from the sentry box to
another crack which is climbed for 25ft. to a stance.
Continue up the crack by layback to another stance and
piton belay below a groove.   3) 45ft. The groove is started
from the left and then followed direct with difficulty to the
top. If the groove is wet the crack on the left can be

19 Winter climbing on Gable Crag

climbed, followed by a short arete to the top of the crag.
Descent: Follow a rake slanting down to the right (looking
out) to the top of the chimney which forms the east edge of
the Slabs. Traverse round to the right and descend a steep
grass slope. Traverse back left to a small col by a pinnacle,
then down a gully to the foot of the Slabs.

47 **The Tomb** ** XS
235ft. *A. G. Cram and W. Young 1966*
An impressive climb which ascends the wall on the right
of Engineer's Slabs. Start 10ft. right of the latter route.
1) 60ft. Traverse right to gain a small sentry box, then
climb straight up to a ledge and belay. 2) 65ft. Move
left and climb the wall for 20ft. on small holds. Then either
move right and climb directly up the wall with the aid of
a peg under the overlap, or traverse left and climb the edge
of the wall until it is possible to traverse back right. Both
routes lead to a good runner. Traverse right to a crack
which is climbed with one peg for aid to a good stance.
3) 110ft. Continue up the groove to an overhang then
move left across the wall to gain a bottomless groove.
Climb this to the top.

48 **The Slant** * HVS
150ft. *M. Burbage, L. J. Griffin, P. L. Fearnehough
and G. Oliver 1968*
A short but well-worthwhile climb. It lies on the small,
steep buttress well to the left of Engineer's Slabs. It is best
reached by scrambling up a scree gully 100yds. to the west
of Windy Gap and striking rightwards when the buttress
comes into view. Start below the left-hand end of the
prominent rightwards-sloping slab.
1) 100ft. The short steep wall and cracked bulge give
access to the slab. Follow this on good holds to the foot
of a steep crack. This leads via a difficult move into a
V-groove, which is left for a slab on the right. A stance
and thread belay are reached below a large overhang.
2) 50ft. Traverse left below the overhang to reach a
deep-cut groove, and follow this strenuously to the top.

20 Looking down the impressive final groove of Engineer's Slabs

WINTER CLIMBING

If good snow and ice conditions are to be found, then this area has some very good climbs to offer. Because of the possibility of variable conditions, the grades given below are only approximate.

Scafell: There are four classic winter gullies; Mickledore Chimney (Grade I), Moss Ghyll (Grade II–III) with the Collie Step as the normal crux, Steep Ghyll (Grade III–IV) usually with a long hard pitch and Deep Ghyll (Grade I–II).

Pike's Crag: Exceptionally can give good gully climbs in the range Grade I to Grade II. After heavy snowfall Pike's Crag may come into condition sooner than Scafell.

Great End: See Borrowdale section.

The Napes: A selection of easy gullies, very rarely in good condition because of the lower altitude and the southerly aspect.

Gable Crag: Often in good condition as the crag faces north, with a variety of worthwhile gullies and ridges in the range Grade I to Grade II. The summer descent from Engineer's Slabs can be a good winter climb (Grade II). The first large gully to the right of Engineer's Slabs, Central Gully (VD), also gives a good winter climb at about Grade II.

21 Opposite: On the crux of the Tomb, Gable Crag

22 Overleaf left: Starting Deep Ghyll, Scafell, with the Pinnacle looming above

23 Overleaf right: Deep Ghyll, Scafell

ESKDALE AND DUDDON

These two quiet valleys have much in common and it is convenient to describe them jointly. Both valleys form convenient bases for the southern and western Lake District, since with motor transport it is possible to reach Wasdale, Langdale and Coniston in about half an hour. As well as these centres, Eskdale itself has two major crags and several smaller ones, whilst Duddon has one crag which is quick-drying and near the road, offering good climbing when the higher crags are out of condition. Duddon has also many short buttresses giving some pleasant outcrop climbs.

Access
Eskdale and Duddon are two roughly parallel valleys separated by a relatively low area of higher ground. The two are connected by Hardknott Pass (1 in 3: no caravans or nervous drivers!) and by the road over Birker Fell between Ulpha and Eskdale Green. Access by road is via the coast road to the south-west or via Wrynose pass from the east. In the summer months a picturesque miniature railway runs between Ravenglass (B.R. station) and Dalegarth near Boot in Eskdale. The nearest railway station to Duddon is Foxfield, also on the coastal line. There is a Mountain Goat Minibus service (twice a day from May to September) from Ambleside via Cockley Beck to Eskdale, and a post bus service between Cockley Beck and Broughton.

Accommodation and Camping
There is a campsite at Boot, and at Brotherilkeld Farm at the head of Eskdale; in Duddon sites can be found at Hall Dunnerdale (215955) and at Turner Hall (233964). Those prepared to carry their tents some distance will find some excellent sites in upper Eskdale below Esk Buttress. There are several inns, guest houses, and farmhouses offering accommodation in both valleys. Youth Hostels can be found at Black Hall Farm (238011) in Duddon and near the head of Eskdale (195010). The Outward Bound have a school in Eskdale Green, and there is a Rucksack Club hut near Turner Hall in Duddon.

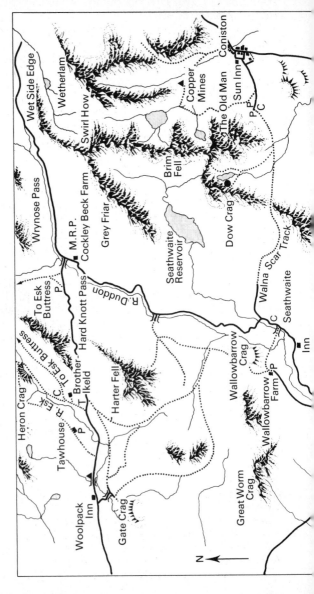

Wet Side Edge

Wetherlam

Swirl How

Coniston

Copper Mines

The Old Man

Sun Inn

P. C

Wrynose Pass

Cockley Beck Farm

M.R.P.

Grey Friar

Brim Fell

Seathwaite Reservoir

Dow Crag

To Esk Buttress

P.

Hard Knott Pass

R. Duddon

Walna Scar Track

Seathwaite

To Esk Buttress

C.

Brother-Ikeld

Harter Fell

C

Wallowbarrow Crag

Inn

Heron Crag

R. Esk

Tawhouse

P.

Wallowbarrow Farm

P

Wallowbarrow Crag

Woolpack Inn

Gate Crag

Great Worm Crag

N ←

52

Food and Drink
Many of the farms and guest houses in the area serve
meals and snacks, and food and drink can be found at the
Woolpack Inn (190010) in Eskdale and the Newfield Hotel
(227960) in Duddon, the latter being especially
recommended. In addition there are other inns in Boot
and Eskdale Green (licensing hours 11–3, 5.30–10.30,
S. 12–2, 7–10.30) and a licensed restaurant at Boot. There
are shops and a PO in Boot, Eskdale Green (EC Sat.) and
Ulpha, with larger shops in Gosforth and Broughton.

Garages
There is a garage in Eskdale Green with a breakdown
service (Eskdale 239), open until 5.30 for repairs and
7 p.m. for petrol. In Duddon some petrol pumps can be
found in Hall Dunnerdale, and there is a service station in
Broughton-in-Furness. The nearest taxi service is at
Gosforth (tel. 225): car hire at Whitehaven (see Wasdale)
and Ulverston (see Coniston).

General Services
Public telephones in Boot, Eskdale Green, Ulpha, Hall
Dunnerdale, also one at the head of Eskdale at the foot of
Hardknott pass. Public toilets at Eskdale Green and
Broughton. Broughton has also a climbing equipment shop
(open on Sundays).

Mountain Rescue
For assistance telephone the POLICE. There is an MR
post at Eskdale Outward Bound School (143002, tel.
Eskdale 281). In addition there is a First Aid post at
Cockley Beck Farm (247017, Thomas Stretcher, no
telephone) and an unmanned post at the top of Mickledore
on Scafell (210068) for Esk Buttress.

ESK BUTTRESS   (223064, called Dow Crag by the
Ordnance Survey)
This fine crag lies on the south flank of Scafell Pike. A
combination of sound clean rock, southern aspect, and
relatively low altitude, make this crag an attractive prospect
at most times of the year. Despite its isolated position the
crag has become very popular in recent years. There is an

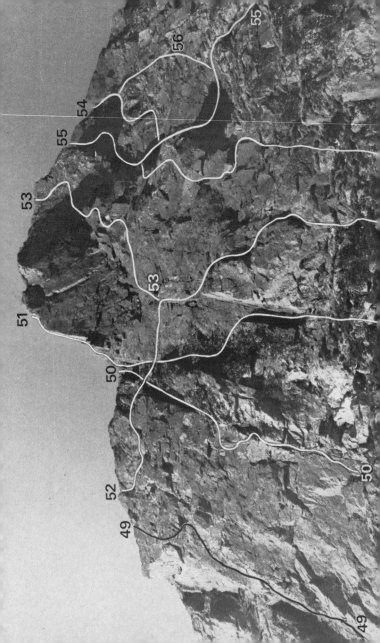

excellent selection of climbs and the crag is well-known for its incut holds.

Approach: The easiest approach is from Eskdale. Park near the foot of Hardknott Pass and follow either the Taw House farm track on the west bank of the river, or the Brotherilkeld path on the east bank and cross the river by a footbridge to join the west bank path past Taw House. Immediately after crossing Cowcove Beck (stone bridge) strike up the fellside via a good zigzag path. The path continues across a plateau and after some miles Upper Eskdale is reached. Continue up the valley past some large boulders (excellent bivouac sites) and the waterfall of Cam Spout to reach the crag. A fairly fit party will do this in 1½ hours or less. In mist, stick to the path which follows the Esk Valley; slightly longer.

The approach from Wasdale is common with the Scafell approach to the top of Mickledore, then descend the Eskdale side for 500ft. and slant left across the fell side to the top of the crag. 1¾ hours, with a steep ascent on the return journey.

From Duddon or Langdale it is usual to motor to Cockley Beck Bridge and walk up Mosedale. From the head of Mosedale descend slightly and cross Lingcove Beck, then contour round under Gait Crags and across the marshy Esk valley to the foot of the crag. This takes about 1¾ hours.

Finally, the approach from Seathwaite in Borrowdale up Grains Ghyll and over Esk Hause takes about 2 hours.

Descent: Slant down the left side (south-west). Various routes, some involving scrambling, join the stream which bounds the Cam Spout side of the crag.

49 **The Red Edge** ** XS
240ft. *J. A. Austin, N. J. Soper and E. Metcalf 1962*
A steep and exhilarating climb with sufficient holds and adequate protection. The route lies up the shallow groove in the rib bounding the central wall on the left. Start up the well-defined chimney.
1) 40ft. Steep climbing to the foot of the chimney. Belay.
2) 130ft. A magnificent pitch. Pull onto a chockstone in the bed of the chimney then move right to the arete. Gain a

small ledge a few feet higher with difficulty and continue up the shallow groove to a small overhang. Difficulties, though not excessive, are relentless, and there are no resting places. Either climb the overhang, or cross the wall to a hidden spike on the arete and climb this until the groove above the overhang can be regained. Continue up the groove on improving holds to a stance in a corner. 3) 70ft. The twin cracks are climbed for 10ft. Move left round the corner then diagonally up large but dubious flakes to the top of the crag.

50 **Black Sunday** ** HVS

305ft. *J. A. Austin, E. Metcalf and N. J. Soper 1962*
A good climb, which is rather strenuous and needs dry conditions. The route follows an obvious line up a crack and groove between Red Edge and Square Chimney. Start at the foot of the arete below the Red Edge.
1) 115ft. Easy climbing to a bilberry ledge. Move up to a belay below and left of the overhanging crack. 2) 90ft. Climb the strenuous crack, with an exit to the right onto a glacis. Move back into the crack for a few feet until a long step left enables a thin slanting crack to be reached. Climb this with difficulty to a resting place under an overhang. Traverse back right and make an awkward pull round the overhang onto the wall on the right. Follow this to a ledge and belay. 3) 55ft. Ascend the corner crack, then continue to a stance and belay on the left. 4) 45ft. The wall on the left of a mossy groove leads to the top of the crag. Belay 30ft. back.

51 **Square Chimney/Medusa Wall** ** VS

480ft. *R. J. Birkett and L. Muscroft 1947*
A good direct route with exposed and exciting situations. The Square Chimney is a prominent feature of the crag on the lower half of the Central Pillar, just left of centre. Starts at the foot of steep broken rock and vegetation directly below the Chimney.
1) 170ft. Scramble up via ledges, little walls, and steep vegetation to reach a ledge just to the right and below the start of the chimney proper. Many belays *en route*. 2) 100ft. A sustained pitch. Climb easily to the foot of the chimney, which is climbed with difficulty for 40ft. Medium-sized

25 *The lonely leader on The Red Edge, Esk Buttress*

climbers will be able to adopt a back-and-foot position (just) but shorter men will have to bridge (much harder). At this point the left side of the chimney falls away. Fix a good runner in the crack (it is possible to belay here, no stance) and gain a small sloping ledge on the left by an awkward move. Traverse left and up a delicate mossy slab into the corner. Climb this to a small stance and belay.
3) 30ft. Continue up the corner groove, or the rib on the left, to reach a belay on the traverse of Bridge's Route.
4) 40ft. Climb the easy gully above and move out right to a rock ledge below the final tower. Belay on left. 5) 45ft. Take the central of three grooves above to the top of the pinnacle, then move right and up to a good belay and stance in a superb position at the edge of the tower overlooking the central wall. 6) 95ft. Climb the groove above for 15ft., then move right to the rib and climb this to a ledge and belay. Continue up easier rocks, trending right, to the top of the crag.

52 Bridge's Route   ***   HS
410ft.   *A. W. Bridge and party   1932*
A superb route, one of the best of its standard in the Lakes, with sustained and exposed climbing. The rock is clean and the route 'goes' without too much difficulty in the wet. Starts more or less directly below the Square Chimney.
1) 170ft. Scrambling up vegetation and occasional steep little walls leads to a ledge just below and to the right of the base of the Square Chimney. This pitch can be split.
2) 45ft. Take a line of weakness in the steep wall above about 30ft. right of the line of Square Chimney. A grass ledge is reached with belay. 3) 25ft. Climb the crack on the left and follow the flake to a ledge and belay. 4) 45ft. Gain the steep groove above and climb it to the level of a jammed spike. Move right and continue straight up on good holds to a ledge and large belay. 5) 40ft. Make an exposed traverse left to a mossy ledge. Climb the groove on the left to a stance and belay. 6) 40ft. Continue the line of the traverse to a pile of flakes on the corner of the buttress. Small belay. 7) 45ft. Climb the steep mossy groove above to a grassy shelf and belay at the top.

53 Central Pillar   **   XS
495ft.   *P. Crew and M. Owen   1962*

58

The route attempts a direct line up the Central Pillar and is forced onto the right-hand arete at the top. A hard climb with small exposed stances and poor protection, it ranks as one of the most serious undertakings on the Scafell Massif. The first four pitches are shared with Bridge's Route.

5) 70ft. Climb the thin crack above the belay for 15ft. then traverse horizontally right for 25ft. or so, when the steepening wall can be climbed, slightly leftwards with increasing difficulty until a hard move right leads to a poor stance and belays (piton recommended). 6) 40ft. Climb the shallow groove above, swing across right to a small ledge then step back left. A hard move over a small overhang is then made to gain a slab. Move right across this and up to a small stance and sundry spike and piton belays below a corner where all roads seem to end.

7) 70ft. Traverse right in a most exposed position and pull up to a small uncomfortable ledge and piton runner. Above on the left a large dubious block sticks out of the overhanging wall. Surmount the block and wall above to gain a traverse line which leads rightwards to a grassy bay.

8) 30ft. The wide crack in the corner, or alternatively the rib on the left, leads to the top.

54 **Great Central Climb** * VS
525ft. *R. J. Birkett and T. Hill 1945*
Another very long route which attempts to ascend the Central Pillar: this time the climb is forced rightwards to join Bower's Route. Start directly below the Central Pillar.

1) 180ft. Scramble up rock and vegetation to a pinnacle leaning against the bottom of the Pillar proper. 2) 125ft. From the top of the pinnacle move diagonally right to finish on a trio of blocks below a small overhang. Move left below the overhang to gain a groove which is climbed to a small ledge. Continue straight up to a ledge on the left (possible belay), then climb up until it is possible to traverse right to the nose of the buttress. Move up to a stance and belay below twin grooves. 3) 20ft. Move up the left-hand groove then traverse right with difficulty to enter Trespasser Groove above pitch 3.

4) 50ft. Either do pitch 4 of Trespasser Groove (HVS) or abseil 15ft. from the belay to gain a traverse line on the right wall. Cross this to a grass ledge and move up to another grass ledge and thread belay. 5) 70ft. Climb

straight up to a juniper ledge. An overhanging crack is then climbed to the Waiting Room on Bower's Route. 6) 50ft. Frankland's Crack. The impending crack leads via an awkward finish to slabs. Go up to a belay below a wide corner crack. 7) 30ft. The crack.

55 **Trespasser Groove** ** HVS
435ft. *A. R. Dolphin and P. Greenwood 1952*
The route takes the large rightward-facing groove which bounds the Central Pillar on the right. The climbing is fairly strenuous, with several long reaches, but difficulties are well-protected. Starts as for Bower's Route.
1) 100ft. The slabs are climbed from left to right. Finish up a grassy shelf to a sloping heather terrace and block belay. 2) 85ft. Traverse diagonally left to a small ledge. Climb a groove slanting up to the right to grass ledges at the foot of the main groove. Piton belay. 3) 90ft. Climb the slab until it is possible to move left into the corner, which is ascended to a recess. The bulge above is awkward, but by bridging up as far as possible on the left it is possible to reach good holds. Spike belay. 5) 40ft. The steep right wall of the groove is climbed with difficulty, starting with an awkward mantelshelf. A traverse right from a flake leads to a good ledge and belays. 6) 40ft. Move back left and climb the corner to the overhang. Make a long reach right to a small hold and swing across on this to better holds. Ascend to a large ledge (the Waiting Room). 7) 50ft. Frankland's Crack. Climb the slightly overhanging crack on the left with an awkward finish. Above, easy slabs lead left to a belay. 8) 30ft. Another steep crack leads strenuously to the top of the crag.

56 **Bower's Route** ** HS
415ft. *G. S. Bower, A. W. Wakefield and P. R. Masson 1920*
A very good route, the easiest way up steep ground; perhaps not quite as good as Bridge's but a little harder, especially the chimney above the Waiting Room. Starts below a sweep of slabs reached by going up a slanting grass rake for 6oft. from the scree at the right-hand edge of the crag.
1) 100ft. The slabs are climbed from left to right finishing

25 *Central Pillar, Esk Buttress. Party in background on Bridge's Route*

up a grassy rake to a sloping heather terrace and block belay. 2) 35ft. Traverse diagonally up to the left to a small ledge. 3) 60ft. Climb a groove which slants up to the right, starting to the right of the belay, to grass ledges and a belay at the foot of a prominent steep crack. 4) 60ft. The crack is ascended using excellent holds and jams. Belay up on the left. 5) 50ft. Steep climbing leads to a ledge. Continue up over a nose followed by a traverse left to a large ledge, the Waiting Room. 6) 50ft. A chimney starts at the right-hand end of the ledge. Some thought is required to start the chimney, and the embarrassing lack of holds continues for several moves. Continue up the V-chimney above until a rock ledge on the right can be gained. Flake belay high up. 7) 60ft. Climb slabs on the right, getting easier, to the top.

HERON CRAG (222030)
An impressive crag with 250ft. of steep compact rock.
All the routes except those on the right flank dry quickly after rain, and the low altitude means the crag is often in condition when the high crags are not.
Approach: Park near the foot of Hardknott Pass and follow the farm tracks on either side of the river. If the west bank path is taken, keep to the Throstle Garth path, and when the path begins to dip down towards the river follow a narrower track on the left which leads eventually to the foot of the crag ($\frac{1}{2}$ hour).
Descent: Down the slopes at the left-hand (south-west) end of the crag.

57 **Side Track** VS
180ft. *R. B. Evans and I. F. Howell 1960*
The buttress to the left of Gormenghast is seamed with grooves and slabs and has a conspicuous line of overlaps slanting left from near the foot of the deep chimney immediately left of Gormenghast (Babylon HS). This delicate climb follows the slab under the overlaps. Start below the tree-filled chimney of Babylon.
1) 35ft. Easily up to a tree at the foot of the chimney.
2) 75ft. Move up to a ledge on the left then traverse left below the overhangs until it is possible to move up into a groove (runner). Traverse left out of the groove onto the

27 *Heron Crag, Eskdale*

63

rib and ascend this to a small stance. 3) 30ft. Continue
straight up to a large oak belay. 4) 40ft. The very steep
wall is climbed via a shallow scoop. Exit right from the
scoop on small holds and finish up a loose groove.

58 **Gormenghast** *** HVS
250ft. *L. Brown and A. L. Atkinson 1960*
A superb route which takes the impressive central pillar of
the crag. One of the best climbs of its grade on sound,
clean rock. Difficulties are nowhere excessive and protection
is good. Starts to the right of the tree-filled groove which
bounds the central pillar on the left.
1) 40ft. Climb the steep wall directly to a good ledge and
piton belay below an obvious overhanging crack. 2) 110ft.
Move 10ft. left and ascend the impending wall on widely
spaced holds until it is possible to traverse back into the
crack. Climb the crack and continue up the groove above
to a stance and belay on a holly. 3) 100ft. Move right
from the tree and ascend on good holds past a block.
Follow a crack, then go straight up the wall on small holds
until better holds lead right to a good ledge. Climb the
bulging rock above on good holds to the top.

59 **Bellerophon** *** VS
185ft. *O. R. D. Pritchard and B. S. Schofield 1958*
A highly enjoyable climb, which follows the deep groove
on the right of the central pillar. Although rather mossy
it can be climbed in wet conditions.
1) 40ft. Climb the arete on the left of the chimney to a
good ledge and belay. 2) 40ft. Move right and climb the
steep crack to enter the big groove. Belay on a large grass
ledge. 3) 45ft. Climb the mossy corner until a step left
leads to a stance and belay on top of a pinnacle. 4) 60ft.
Go straight up for 20ft. then traverse left to an enormous
bird's nest. A shallow groove slanting left finishes the climb.

60 **Spec Crack** * XS
215ft. *P. Walsh, J. A. Austin and E. Metcalf 1961*
A good route up the mossy wall to the right of Bellerophon.
The overhang is hard and strenuous but well-protected:
the rest is delicate, steep climbing up mossy rock. Starts

28 *Pulling over the overhang on Spec Crack, Heron Crag*

30ft. to the right of Bellerophon.

1) 8oft. Climb the wall to the overhang (runner) and pull over into the crack above with difficulty. Continue up the crack to a holly tree belay. 2) 40ft. Ascend the crack on the right to a small stance below an overhanging crack. 3) 65ft. Climb the crack until it is necessary to break out on the left wall. Go up this to a small stance. 4) 30ft. Continue up another crack to the top.

WALLOWBARROW CRAG (222966, called Low Crag by the Ordnance Survey)

This pleasant crag has a variety of short but interesting routes. Some important points in its favour are that it dries out very quickly after rain, faces south-west, and lies at a low altitude. Many a wet weekend at Wasdale has been saved by a sudden change in the weather and a visit to Wallowbarrow on the way home.

Access: By road from the bridge over the river Duddon, about one mile south-west of Seathwaite. Take a narrow lane past the petrol pumps and park near High Wallowbarrow Farm. From here it is 10 minutes walk to the crag. On foot from Seathwaite take a path starting near the church and cross the Duddon by a footbridge (note the first crossing is Tarn Beck) to High Wallowbarrow Farm.

Descent: The crag is split into two buttresses, West and East, by a dirty loose gully. Descend from the West Buttress to the left (west) and from the East Buttress to the right.

61 **Bryanston** * VS

18oft. *J. Smith 1956*

A good climb up the centre of the West Buttress with a steep and exhilarating final pitch. Starts in the centre of the foot of the buttress.

1) 8oft. Climb a broken rib to a stance and large flake belay in a recess on the left. 2) 55ft. Move right and ascend diagonally rightwards for 30ft. Traverse horizontally right and go up to a small stance and belay below and right of a steep crack. 3) 45ft. Climb the crack. The initial move is awkward and the rest steep but the holds are excellent. When the crack ends move left and continue to the top on large holds.

62 **Thomas** HS

16oft. *W. F. Dowlen and D. Stroud* *1955*

Another good climb which takes the clean rib on the right-hand side of the West Buttress. Starts just left of the foot.

1) 7oft. Ascend a groove slanting right, then straight up to below some perched blocks. Step right and climb to a ledge with a tree belay on the left. 2) 6oft. Move back right onto the face and go up the steep cracked wall to a large ledge at the top of the ridge. 3) 3oft. Traverse the wall on the right for a few feet then ascend the steep and awkward wall direct to the top.

63 **Digitation** MVS

175ft. *D. G. Heap, J. R. Amatt and C. B. Greenhalgh* *1963*

An enjoyable route up the slabs on the right side of the East Buttress. Starts at a block lying against the face and directly below a large oak.

1) 35ft. Climb the block and the slab above to a ledge and belay on the right. 2) 8ft. Step left and ascend the shallow groove to a small overhang (runner). Pull over leftwards (awkward) and continue up on better holds to a large grass ledge and oak tree. 3) 6oft. Climb the steep wall behind the ledge until it is possible to move easily into the corner on the left. Follow the corner to the top.

64 **Cornflake** * VS

2ooft. *M. Thompson, F. Draper and J. Lindsey* *1966*

A good route, continuously steep and exciting despite the break at half height. Lies on a buttress below and to the east of Wallowbarrow, about 1ooyd. upstream from the footbridge across the Duddon between Wallowbarrow Farm and Seathwaite. Starts at a block below a cleaned rib.

1) 3oft. Step off the block and climb the rib to a ledge and tree belay. 2) 7oft. Climb the slab right of the corner and continue up past a ledge and an oak on steep rocks until it is possible to traverse left to the foot of an impending V-groove. The lower section of the groove is rather blank but good holds are soon reached and the top gained. Scramble up an extra 2oft. to a belay. Walk 5oft. right along the terrace to the foot of a wide flake crack curving up to the left. 3) 1ooft. Climb the crack and make an exciting hand traverse along the crest of the flake to a niche.

Gain the top of the flake and step into the groove above. Follow this to a grass ledge, then cross a mossy slab to the right and continue up easier ground to the top. Descend the crag to the west.

WINTER CLIMBING
Due to the relatively low altitude of the crags in this area there is little of interest except in a very hard winter. There are short gullies on the crags overlooking Seathwaite Tarn in the Duddon Valley, and in Eskdale the crags below the ridge joining Slight Side to Scafell may offer some short climbs. The head of Little Narrowcove on Scafell Pike may also have some short routes.

Coniston is a useful centre for the southern Lake District but tends to get very crowded at peak holiday times. The main climbing attraction here is Dow Crag, with a variety of big mountain routes and many shorter problems. In addition there are several smaller crags round Levers Water and elsewhere which offer numerous shorter climbs in pleasant surroundings, despite the old mine workings and the expanding quarry activities. The area is shown on the Eskdale and Duddon map.

Access

By road from Greenodd to the south, Ambleside to the east, and from Duddon (via Wrynose pass) from the west. There is a frequent bus service from Ambleside and weekday service from Ulverston, the nearest railway station. Those on foot approaching from the Duddon Valley can take the pleasant Walna Scar road.

Accommodation and Camping

The official camp site is at Lands Point, south of Coniston village near the Lake (304964), but some good sites can be found below Coniston Old Man on the Walna Scar road (up the steep hill behind the disused station, then follow an unmetalled road for about half a mile to just past the point where a steep road goes up to a quarry on the right, (282968). A good bivouac site can be found in some large boulders in the scree below Dow Crag.

There are many hotels and guest houses in Coniston village and also some inns and guest houses in Torver to the south. There is a Youth Hostel in the village (Far End, 302980) and another in the Coppermines Valley (289986). In addition there are many small club huts in the area.

Food and Drink

Coniston is well equipped with hotels, cafés and pubs. The nearest bar to the crags is in the Sun Inn (300975) just below the disused railway station. Licensing hours are 11–3, 5.30–10.30, S. 12–2, 7–10.30. There are several shops in Coniston, early closing days Thurs./Sat. Torver has some pleasant inns.

Garages and Car Hire

There is a garage in Coniston with repair and breakdown services up to 5 pm, tel. Coniston 253. Petrol sales continue until 8 pm. The nearest car hire is at Ulverston, tel. 52020,

or Windermere, tel. 2580. Taxis at Ulverston 53962 and 52135; Windermere 2355.

General Services

Public toilets can be found in Coniston, and there are public telephones in Coniston and Torver. The nearest equipment shops are in Ambleside, 7 miles away.

Mountain Rescue

There is a manned post in Coniston at Dow Crag House (305976), tel. Coniston 330. In addition there is an unmanned post at the foot of Dow Crag (263979). For assistance go to the rescue post or telephone the POLICE, whichever is quicker.

DOW CRAG (263978)

Dow Crag is the most readily accessible big mountain crag for those approaching the Lake District from the south. Since it has a good variety of long climbs it has always been a popular pilgrimage for those aspiring to Higher Things. The rock is sound and compact and gives enjoyable climbing in good conditions, but when wet can resemble verglas in texture and temperature. If the prevailing wind is from the north the crag feels much colder than its altitude would suggest.

Access

From Coniston, take the road up the steep hill behind the disused railway station and follow the unmetalled road (the Walna Scar road) below Coniston Old Man. Shortly after passing through two rock gateways a path leaves the track on the right. Follow this, passing below some old quarries on the west flank of the Old Man, and round a rocky spur to reach Goat's Water. The crag lies above the tarn and is reached by a steep diagonal ascent up the scree. The crag can also be reached from Torver by a path crossing the Walna Scar road just above the rock gateways. From the Duddon Valley, follow the Walna Scar road to the watershed, and take the ridge over Brown Pike and Buck Pike to the top of the crag.

Descent: For those climbs which finish at the top of the crag, the best descent is on the left (south) down a slanting

29 *Dow Crag*
    E = Easy Terrace, used for descent

scree rake to the south of Easy Gully. Easy Gully, which bounds 'A' Buttress on the left, is another possible descent route but one not recommended in the presence of other parties due to the danger of rockfall. Most of the routes on 'B' and 'C' buttresses finish on Easy Terrace, and the best descent from this is on the left (some scrambling, awkward in the dark or in bad conditions).

65 Arete, Chimney and Crack   MS

36oft.   *T. C. Ormiston-Chant, T. M. G. Parker and S. H. Gordon 1910*

A long and interesting route, marred slightly by a broken middle section. Start at the lowest point of the left-hand side of 'A' Buttress.

1) 7oft. Climb the Arete on good holds to a rock ledge. Continue up the wall with increasing difficulty to an overhung ledge.   2) 35ft. Move left and up a crack to large block belays.   3) 7oft. Easy grass and rock slanting right to a recess of blocks.   4) 25ft. Move right to below the chimney.   5) 3oft. The Chimney, passing an awkward chockstone.   6) 4oft. The exposed ledge is traversed to the right to below a chimney-crack.   7) 9oft. The Crack is exposed but furnished with good holds all the way to the top.

66 Gordon and Craig's Route   **   HVD

31oft.   *S. H. Gordon, A. Craig and party 1909*

A very good climb of its standard, tracing the easiest way up the buttress. Care is required in the choice of belays, as there has been at least one serious accident on the upper section of the climb. Start at a scoop sloping left some 4oft. up to the right from the start of Arete, Chimney and Crack. Many scratches hereabouts.

1) 45ft. The scoop leads to a good belay.   2) 35ft. Step left and move up to ledges leading left to join Arete, Chimney and Crack.   3)–6) 165ft. As for the same pitches of the previous climb.   7) 2oft. Follow a slab from the right-hand end of the traverse into a niche.   8) 4oft. Continue up to the right to a ledge of blocks and climb an exposed crack to a ledge. This pitch is the hardest on the climb. Scramble up left to the summit ridge.

30 Isengard, Dow Crag

67 **Isengard** * HVS

175ft.   *L. Brown and A. McHardy   1962*

A very interesting variation to Eliminate 'A', taking a vague crack line to gain the cave of Eliminate 'A' from below. Start 15ft. left of Eliminate 'A'.

1) 25ft. The crack leads to small ledges and poor belays on a slab.   2) 80ft. Climb the steepening slab, bearing left until a hard move over a bulge leads to a traverse line crossing the buttress. Move right along the ledge to a belay behind a large flake.   3) 70ft. Move back left to the foot of a bulging crack. This is climbed acrobatically to a spike. Better holds lead to an overlap which guards the slabby floor of the cave (thread runner on left). Pull over the overhang onto the slab and move up to a belay and junction with Eliminate 'A'. Continue up Eliminate 'A'.

68 **Eliminate 'A'** *** VS

375ft.   *H. S. Gross, G. Basterfield   1923*

A magnificent route wending its way up the walls and overhangs of the right-hand side of the Buttress. All difficulties are adequately protected. Start at a grassy ledge at the foot of the right-hand side of the buttress overlooking Great Gully.

1) 45ft. A spiral ascent to the right is made until a crack containing a loose spike can be climbed onto a grass ledge with belay 8ft. above.   2) 60ft. Mantelshelf onto the belay, and continue up a line of scoops and grooves to a recess under an overhang. Move awkwardly left onto a slab and up on better holds to a good ledge and belay.   3) 15ft. Move round to the right and up to an overhung block ledge.

4) 50ft. The Rochers Perchés pitch. (The blocks which gave the pitch its name have long since disappeared.) Move left onto the wall (peg) and make an awkward move onto a small ledge in the corner. Step down to the left to a good thread to protect the second, and cross a slab to a belay in The Cave.   5) 55ft. Follow the exposed flake up to the left and up a short chimney to a good ledge and belays.

6) 65ft. An exposed pitch. Traverse right across a delicate slab to the foot of a shallow groove which leads on good holds to the Gordon and Craig Traverse.   7) 85ft. The crack is climbed to the top, or, more difficult but distinctly artificial, climb a shallow groove 12ft. left of the crack and step right to a flake almost in the crack. Climb the

overhang and a shallow groove leading leftwards to the top.

69 **Sidewalk** * XS

275ft. *L. Brown and B. Stevens 1960*

This formidable climb traces a line up the right-hand arete of 'A' Buttress overlooking Great Gully. Although the first pitch is the hardest, the climb remains serious and exposed right to the top. Start from the top of the first pitch of Great Gully.

1) 20ft. Move left into an impending scoop and climb up to a small grass ledge. Desperate! 2) 30ft. The corner crack is smooth and strenuous but short. A good ledge on Eliminate 'A' is reached. 3) 50ft. Move right below the steep wall and pull over a tiny overhang to gain a shallow corner (runners). Step out right into the prominent dogleg crack and move up to an exposed ledge. 4) 70ft. Go up easier ground above trending first right then left to a belay below the shallow groove. Care is required with loose blocks on this and the next pitch. 5) 105ft. Climb the shallow groove to the overhang and follow the slanting crack out to the left to the top of the crag.

70 **Giant's Crawl** ** D

420ft. *E. T. W. and D. T. Addyman, X. Stobart 1909*

A fine climb which takes the band of slabs which crosses the steep upper half of 'B' buttress in a diagonal line from the foot of Great Gully. Starts immediately right of the foot of the Gully.

1) 60ft. Climb easy slabs and traverse left along a narrow ledge to the foot of a crack. 2) 80ft. Go up the crack for 30ft., then continue up the slab to a good rock ledge. Walk up to the right to reach belays. 3) 30ft. Easily up for a few feet then more slab climbing on the left to another ledge and small belays. 4) 90ft. Continue up the slabs above, taking a central line and passing ledges with poor belays. A large grass ledge overlooking Easy Terrace is reached (possible escape by traversing down to the right to reach the Terrace). 5) 40ft. Traverse a ledge to the left to reach the foot of an overhanging corner. 6) 60ft. Climb the difficult crack up the corner to a good ledge. Walk round to the left to another crack in a steep groove, which has better holds and leads to a belay on the right. 7) 60ft. Easier climbing and scrambling leads to the top.

71 **Nimrod** ** XS
250ft.   *D. Miller and D. Kirby   1962*
Although artificial in its line, the climbing on this varied
route is both hard and sustained. The first two pitches lie
up the steep walls below the slab of Giant's Crawl. Start
up a shallow groove at the left end of the wall and above
the foot of Easy Terrace.
1) 100ft. Gain the groove from the right and climb it to a
small overhang. This is overcome using doubtful flakes and
a long delicate traverse is then made to the right (poor
protection) to the foot of a shallow groove. The best stance
is 10ft. below.   2) 50ft. Climb the right wall of the groove
until the wall steepens then make a committing move into
the groove. More hard moves then lead to the slab of
Giant's Crawl.   3) 100ft. Move across the slabs to the foot
of an open corner. Climb this with difficulty to a small
ledge and continue up a thin crack to a very small spike.
With aid from the rope traverse left to an arete and move
up to a small ledge. Turn an overhang on the left and
move up to easy ground.

72 **Leopard's Crawl** * HVS
160ft.   *R. J. Birkett, L. Muscroft and T. Hill   1947*
This very open climb takes the steep wall below the final
crack of Murray's Route. Poor protection and sustained
climbing combine to make it unusually serious for its
length. Start at a bridged block midway between the
stretcher box and the foot of Easy Rake.
1) 90ft. Pull onto the wall above the block, make a slightly
descending hand traverse to the right and move up into
a shallow groove (poor runners). Traverse very delicately
across the slab to a niche below a shallow groove, and go
up this to a good ledge below the last pitch of Murray's
Route.   2) 70ft. Traverse right for 15ft. and climb a
shallow groove to the top of the crag, and Easy Terrace.

72A **Tarkus/Catacomb** XS
380ft.   *R. B. Matheson and M. R. Matheson   1972*
A good combination which is both delicate and strenuous.
Protection is adequate but not always easy to arrange. Starts
just below the bridged block of Leopard's Crawl.

31 *Leopard's Crawl, Dow Crag*

1) 110ft. The objective is a hidden flake crack 15ft. to the right. This is best reached by moving up then making a descending traverse with the aid of a small flake. Go up the wall, slightly leftwards, to a horizontal break and better holds. Traverse right to a sentry box then climb the impending groove to a spike. Continue straight up the delicate wall and easier crack to join Murray's Route. 2) 70ft. Traverse right for 15ft and climb a shallow groove to the top, and Easy Terrace (pitch 2 of Leopard's Crawl). Scramble over easy ledges to below an obvious traverse line below the overhangs, high on the steep wall well right of Nimrod. Start at the foot of a wide crack at the upper end of the upper terrace (Hyacinth Terrace). 3) 100ft. Climb the crack, steep then overhanging then move left using good flake holds to an overhung gangway. Follow this then hand-traverse to a ledge. Go diagonally left to a horizontal fault leading to Giant's Crawl. 4) 50ft. Go beneath the overhang and along the obvious traverse left to a large grass ledge. Peg belays. 5) 50ft. Start on the right, using a peg to step onto the wall above an overlap. Move left and then right, following the crack to the top.

73 **Murray's Route** *** S   18·3·85 + Granny Moss
250ft. *D. G. Murray, W. J. Borrowman and B. L. Martin 1918*
A magnificent route, one of the best of its standard in the Lakes. It takes a generally leftward-trending line up 'B' buttress, starting just left of the stretcher box.
1) 65ft. Climb the deep V-chimney to the overhang. Move out left across a very polished slab (good fingerholds in the crack) to a resting place, then move up to a position below the overhang. Pass this on the left with difficulty and move up into the big corner. 2) 55ft. Go diagonally right over a perched flake and move up the arete to the left of a chimney. Step into the chimney and climb up to a deep cave. 3) 35ft. Make a steep pull up a crack above the chimney and cross a big flake to a ledge in the corner, above the first stance. 4) 35ft. The V-chimney on the left is followed by an exposed traverse along another flake to a stance below the final crack. 5) 60ft. The very smooth ! crack leads to the top.

32 *Murray's Route, Dow Crag*

74 **Murray's Direct**   ** VS
155ft.   *Various parties   1922–1945*
A series of variations on Murray's route which gives a
sustained direct route up the buttress. Starts at a vertical
embedded flake 40ft. left of the start of Murray's Route.
1) 40ft. Tiger Traverse. From the top of the flake move onto
the wall and traverse round to the right until the slanting
slab can be gained. Follow this delicately to the right to
ledges, belay on higher ledges on a large flake on the right.
2) 35ft. Climb the steep wall above the large flake, moving
left to a stance below a vertical layback crack.   3) 80ft. Move
up into the corner and climb the crack for 15ft. to good
footholds. Continue up the crack to below the large
overhang and traverse right to the foot of another crack.
Climb this to a grass ledge, then scrambling leads to
Easy Terrace.

75 **Abraham's Route**   S   *18-3-85 + heavy moss*
255ft.   *G. D. and A. P. Abraham and F. T. Phillipson   1903*
A pleasant route with an interesting final pitch. Starts up
a grassy groove at the foot of the buttress.
G 1) 45ft. Climb the groove, past grass ledges, to a recess
with a belay on the right. L 2) 35ft. Step back across the
groove and continue until it is possible to traverse 10ft. left to
a belay below a steep wall. G 3) 45ft. Ascend the open
groove in the steep wall above. The climbing eases after 20ft.
and eventually the left end of a long ledge is reached.
L 4) 60ft. Climb slabs on the right and continue to below an
impending wall, with a large belay on the right. G 5) 70ft.
Descend to the left for about 30ft., until a difficult move can
be made to cross the sloping rib on the left to reach a sloping
foothold. Continue up the slab above to reach a small spike,
then move left again and climb an easier slab and broken
ground to reach Easy Terrace.

76 **Woodhouse's Route**   * HVD
190ft.   *G. F. and A. J. Woodhouse   1905*
A polished and strenuous route, especially in wet conditions.
Fortunately the pitches are short and the stances large.
Starts by scrambling up towards Central Chimney for 100ft.
to the foot of a wide groove below and to the left of the large

33 Murray's Direct, Dow Crag

pinnacle set in the left wall of the Chimney.

1) 30ft. Climb the groove to the foot of the pinnacle. Follow the wide crack on the left to the crevasse behind the pinnacle.   2) 35ft. Move back left and enter a chimney with difficulty. Climb this with good holds on the left to a ledge and belay. Move left and traverse on grassy ledges to reach a deep recess.   3) 30ft. Climb the polished wall on the left with some help for the right foot from a deep crack.   A problematical pitch, leading to a ledge on the left.   4) 45ft. Ascend the easy arete above the ledge to a large grassy terrace. Walk right to a large block belay below a steep crack.   5) 30ft. Climb the crack, with a difficult start, or alternatively the delicate easy-angled slab running diagonally right below the wall. Follow a crevasse to the right to another steep wall with a projecting block and recess.   6) 20ft. Climb the wall left of the block with difficulty.

77 **Central Chimney**   *   MS
130ft.   *O. G. Jones and G. Ellis   1897*
Takes the corner crack between 'B' buttress and 'C' buttress, with a steep left wall and a slabby right wall. Scramble up broken ground for 100ft. from the path to the foot of the corner proper.

1) 35ft. The first 20ft. is climbed using large wedged flakes. The remainder of the pitch is much smoother and is climbed with the left foot in the crack. Traverse right from a recess for 10ft. to a ledge and flake belay.   2) 40ft. Move back and climb the Chimney, using the right wall, to reach another recess with small belays on the right.   3) 55ft. Take to the rib on the right and climb on good holds to a small flat ledge, then continue up to the cave with more difficulty. Bridge up the cave until the left wall can be gained and good holds lead to the top. Easy Terrace can be reached by scrambling up to the left.

78 **'C' Ordinary Route**   ***   D
36oft.   *G. F. and A. J. Woodhouse   1904*
A worthwhile route in all weather conditions, particularly suitable for beginners. Starts just left of the foot of 'C' Buttress.

34 *Eliminate 'C', Dow Crag*

1) 50ft. Climb the crest of the buttress to a narrow ledge on top of a large flake. 2) 55ft. Go up to a small ledge and follow the polished slabby scoop above to easier ground and ledges. A good ledge with a fallen flake is reached. 3) 35ft. Climb an open scoop, starting from the left end of the ledge, to another ledge on the right. 4) 35ft. Ascend easy rocks leftwards to a ledge on the corner of the buttress. 5) 25ft. Climb the corner of the buttress or an easier groove on the right to a ledge. 6) 50ft. Move right and ascend to a smooth slab which is followed to a large ledge. A ledge with better belays is reached up on the right. 7) 45ft. Traverse left for 10ft. and climb the wall on the left of the crack above. Move left to below a small cave and climb a wide crack to the top of a large flake to the left of the cave. From the top of the flake step up left then back right to a small stance and good belay 10ft. above the flake. 8) 65ft. Traverse slabs to the right to a good ledge. Continue rightwards following a gangway round a bulge to a ledge. A short wall on the left followed by a horizontal traverse leads easily to Easy Terrace.

79 **Eliminate 'C'** MVS
150ft. *H. S. Gross and G. Basterfield 1922*
A good climb in grand surroundings following a line parallel to Intermediate Gully. Start at the top of the second pitch of that climb (the horrors of its first two pitches can be avoided by scrambling on the right). 1) 85ft. A diagonal crack leads out to the left to a small ledge. Step down to the left and then make a delicate move up the arete to a good ledge. Step right and continue up the arete on good holds to a fine stance overlooking the gully. 2) 65ft. On the right is a fine slab undercut at its base. Climb the corner on the left for a few feet then cross the slab on small holds to a very prominent spike. Climb the arete on good holds and finish up a leftward-slanting groove

80 **Intermediate Gully** ** HS
170ft. *E. A. and J. H. Hopkinson and X. Campbell 1895*
One of the finest gully climbs in the district, offering both sustained and strenuous climbing throughout its length on perfect rock. Scramble up the gully for 100ft. until the walls close in. Usually wet. 1) 30ft. A strenuous crack and short chimney, climbed by

its right wall, leads to a comfortable recess and belay.
2) 25ft. Awkward bridging is used to overcome the smooth
chockstone.   3) 70ft. Step left into the steep crack which
leads strenuously to easier rock. When this steepens climb
the left wall to a recess below a large chock.   4) 15ft.
Struggle over the jammed stone to gain a cave.   5) 30ft.
Move up to the right then step left to gain a crack in the
left wall which is followed to Easy Terrace.

81 **Great Central Route**   *   HVS
205ft.   *J. I. Roper, G. S. Bower, and party   1919*
Above the wide funnel of Easter Gully is an amphitheatre
dominated by an imposing pillar. Great Central Route
ascends this pillar. Start by scrambling up Easter Gully into
the amphitheatre to a point just left of the nose of the
pillar.
1) 45ft. Climb the nose and the slabs above to a ledge
below a vertical crack (South America Crack).   2) 35ft.
Gain the crack from the right, and layback to reach the
wider part. Easier climbing leads to the Bandstand.   3) 60ft.
The difficult wall above. Start just left of a slight nose,
then, after a step right, climb to a tiny ledge. Continue up
a crack to a good ledge (runner under overhang). Traverse
left across the slab and move up Broadrick's Crack to belay.
4) 65ft. Move right onto the wall and climb up until it is
possible to gain a ledge on the right. Traverse to the
right-hand end then step down and move round the corner
to a slab. Follow this on good holds to the top.

82 **Hopkinson's Crack**   **   HS
150ft.   *C. Hopkinson and O. Koecher   1895*
A classic crack climb, up the right-hand corner of the
amphitheatre, on clean sound rock. Start by scrambling
up Easter Gully, with one moderate cave pitch, into the
amphitheatre.
1) 50ft. Climb the crack to a good ledge on the left.
Thread belay below the steep crack on the left.   2) 40ft.
Move back into the corner and climb up on decreasing
holds until another ledge on the left leads to a belay.
3) 60ft. Re-enter the crack and climb it to the top. Belay
10ft. up to the right.
The best descent is to traverse left on grass ledges to the
easy upper half of Intermediate Gully which is descended
to Easy Terrace.

WINTER CLIMBING

Despite its cold reputation, Dow Crag is not often in good condition for winter climbing. When conditions are suitable Easy Gully, to the left of 'A' Buttress, gives a relatively easy route, and the other gullies give climbs of varying degrees of difficulty. Some of the easier summer climbs, such as Giant's Crawl, can be exciting winter routes.

This easily-accessible valley runs in a westerly direction
from Ambleside. Famous for its trio of Pikes, it ranks as
the most popular area in the Lake District for both
climbing and walking. Because of this popularity the crags
are often overcrowded, and those preferring peace and quiet
are advised to go elsewhere at peak holiday times. There is
a good selection of both high mountain crags and valley
outcrops, with climbs in all grades. In general the rock is
sound and the protection good, and as many of the crags
face south, they are quick to dry. The more remote Deer
Bield Crag is described in this section also, although it does
not lie in Great Langdale itself.

Access

There is a regular bus service from Ambleside to Langdale.
Cars are still allowed up the valley, though the road is
heavily congested in the summer months and the official
car parks (285061, 285059, 295064) cannot cope, filling
up very quickly. Langdale can also be reached from
Duddon by car, via Wrynose Pass and the Blea Tarn Road.

Accommodation and Camping

Camping is only allowed on the official site at the head of
Langdale (285059), and there are several climbing huts
(F.R.C.C., Wayfarers, Achille Ratti) about a mile from the
valley head at Raw Head (304067) and one (Yorkshire
Ramblers) in Little Langdale (309029). Langdale is well
served with guest houses and hotels, although it is necessary
to book well in advance for peak holiday times. Many
more hotels and guest houses can be found in Ambleside,
7 miles away. There are Youth Hostels at High Close
(338052) and Elterwater (327046) and in Ambleside. There
is an accommodation bureau in Church Street,
Ambleside, tel. 2582.

Food and Drink

Langdale and Ambleside are well provided with places to
eat and drink, although most establishments are tending to
cater more and more for rich tourists and less for penniless
climbers. There are bars at Chapel Stile and the Old and
New Dungeon Ghyll Hotels. The latter also has a cafeteria
which serves meals. As well as the bars mentioned above there
are inns at Little Langdale and Skelwith Bridge. In Ambleside
the Salutation Hotel bar is usually crowded with climbers;

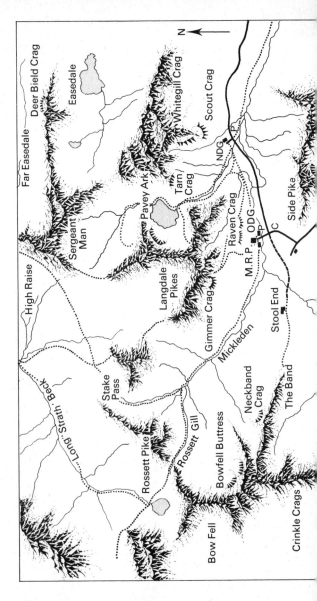

a Lake District version of the Padarn Hotel. Normal
licensing hours 11–3, 5.30–10.30, Sun. 12–2, 7–10.30.
There is a small shop on the Langdale campsite, a PO
and Co-Op. at Chapel Stile, and shops at Elterwater
(EC Sat.) and Ambleside (EC Thurs.)

Garages and Car Hire
There are petrol pumps in Chapel Stile and an AA garage
with 24-hour breakdown service in Ambleside (tel. 3273).
Taxis at Ambleside (tel. 2032 and 2198) and car hire at
Windermere (2580).

General Services
There is a tourist advice bureau in the centre of Ambleside,
and most general services, including equipment shops.
Public toilets can be found at Chapel Stile and telephones
at Chapel Stile, Elterwater and Skelwith Bridge.

Mountain Rescue
For assistance ring the local POLICE (999). There is a
MR post at the Old Dungeon Ghyll Hotel (286061, tel.
Langdale 272), and first aid boxes at the New Dungeon
Ghyll Hotel (295065) and at the Co-Op. in Chapel Stile.

WHITE GHYLL CRAG (298071)

This easily-accessible crag lies some 800 yards NE of the
New Dungeon Ghyll Hotel, and is very obvious as a notch
in the skyline. It provides a number of climbs of about
150–250ft. in length, mainly in the higher standards.
Approach: Use the car park opposite the New Dungeon
Ghyll Hotel. A footbridge behind the hotel is crossed to
reach Mill Ghyll Farm. A path leads first steeply up the
hillside then right over a stile to a wood. Pass below this
to gain the stony bed of the Ghyll. Follow this to the crag.
Descent: The crag is divided by a series of ledges into an
upper and lower section. The ledges (Easy Rake) provide a
convenient means of descent from climbs on the lower
crag and the right-hand section of the upper crag.

83 **Slip Knot** * MVS
150ft. *R. J. Birkett and L. Muscroft 1947*
An interesting climb with very good holds. Starts on the
lower crag directly below a corner, capped by a large
overhang, opposite a sycamore.

35 *White Ghyll, Lower Crag*

1) 85ft. Easy climbing leads to the foot of the corner proper. Follow this for 20ft. then a line of good holds leads out up the right wall to a good ledge below the overhang. Poor belays, piton recommended.   2) 65ft. Traverse left below the overhang into the corner. Move delicately onto the arete and climb this, with an exhilarating move over the bulge, to a niche on the left. A steep wall leads to easy climbing. Easy Rake can be reached by traversing shattered ledges to the left.

84 **Laugh Not**   HVS
115ft.   *J. Brown, R. Moseley and T. Waghorn*   *1953*
This is the open corner to the right of Slip Knot. It is not as steep as that climb, but what it lacks in height and steepness, it makes up in smoothness. The protection is very good. Start by scrambling up to the right from the foot of Slip Knot to the foot of the corner.
1) 115ft. The first few feet of the corner are easy. After a small overhang a finger jamming crack is followed strenuously to a narrow ledge on the left wall. Above this the crack widens and is climbed more easily to a rapidly vanishing tree stump. A few feet higher a crack leads out up the right wall to a ledge below the overhang. From here either step down and cross a blank slab to the arete on the right, or make an alarming hand traverse on the lip to the same point. Take a piton belay immediately to avoid rope drag. The top of Slip Knot is reached by scrambling up to the left.

85 **Hollin Groove**   S   *15/3/85 Gary Moss*
150ft.   *R. J. Birkett and L. Muscroft*   *1945*
A varied and interesting climb taking the conspicuous V-groove 50ft. to the left of the sycamore. Start at the foot of a short steep crack.
L 1) 40ft. The crack is strenuous. At its top move left and up to a stance below a steep wall. *L* 2) 30ft. Move left and up into a groove below a holly. A very steep move to the right on good holds leads to a stance below the main groove. *C* 3) 80ft. The groove is followed to Easy Rake. Scramble up to a belay. The climb can be extended above Easy Rake by climbing the ridge above at VD standard.

86   **White Ghyll Wall**   *   MVS

205ft.   *R. J. Birkett, L. Muscroft and T. Hill   1946*

A fine route, exposed in its upper section. This climb is on the upper crag and starts near a triangular cave some 35ft. left of where Easy Rake runs into the ground.

1) 50ft. The rib on the right of the cave leads to a ledge below a large overhang. (Perhaps Not, a loose HVS, leads across the overhung slab to the left).   2) 30ft. Traverse right to a block belay. (This point can be reached by an easy traverse left from the highest point of Easy Rake, thus providing a useful extension to the climbs on the lower crag).   3) 50ft. An undercut scoop is climbed past a difficult overhang to a good spike. Move diagonally left up the steep wall until a delicate traverse can be made into a hidden groove—belay 10ft. above.   4) 95ft. A diagonal ascent of the slab on the left is followed by easier climbing on good holds to the top of the crag.

87   **Gordian Knot**   **   VS

200ft.   *J. W. Haggas and Miss E. Bull   1940*

A magnificent route breaking through the central overhangs via a hanging corner. Start at the first obvious break to the left of White Ghyll Wall.

1) 60ft. The steepening slab is climbed with increasing difficulty to a niche. Opposing spike belays.   2) 50ft. Traverse easily right to the foot of a steep corner. The first few moves are problematical and lead to a small ledge on the right wall. Good holds lead back into the corner which is followed to a chockstone belay.   3) 80ft. The wide crack is climbed to a good ledge on the right. Continue up the wall above on good holds to the top of the crag.

88   **Haste Not**   **   VS

190ft.   *R. J. Birkett and L. Muscroft   1948*

A climb of sustained interest and spectacular situations. A recess immediately left of Gordian Knot marks the start of the climb.

1) 70ft. The left-hand corner of the recess is climbed to the overhang. Cross the wall on the left, with difficulty, to reach a groove in the slab. The groove is followed via an awkward bulge to a large platform and block belay.   2) 50ft. An exposed traverse is made to the right to a prow. Climb the slab to an overhang (runner) then make a series

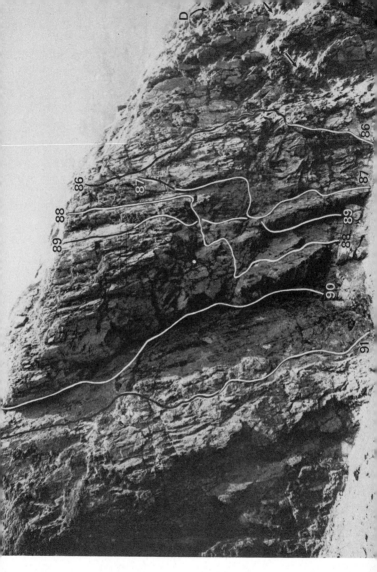

36 *White Ghyll, Upper Crag*
  D = Descent route

93

of sensational moves along a narrow gangway into a groove. Swing round the rib on the right to the ledge above the second pitch of Gordian Knot. Move along the ledge to a belay.   3) 70ft. Move back left and climb the wall above past an inverted V overhang. Easier climbing leads to the top of the crag.

89 **Haste Not Direct**   *   XS
215ft.   *P. Allison and N. Smithers (Pitch 1)   1962*
J. A. Austin and C. E. Davies (Pitch 2)   1965
J. A. Austin and R. Valentine (Pitch 3)   1971
Three fine pitches become increasingly difficult. Starts up the long corner on the right of the normal route.
1) 70ft. Climb the corner to a large roof. Move out right onto the rib and belay on the right as for Gordian Knot.
2) 55ft. Enter the narrow groove above on the left with difficulty, pulling out left to a resting place and peg runner after a few feet. Continue up the slab and overhang to the traverse of Haste Not. Follow this right, across the bottomless groove, to a poor stance and good belay.
3) 30ft. Climb the very strenuous bulging crack above on the left.   4) 60ft. Continue up walls and slabs to the top.

90 **White Ghyll Chimney**   *   S   *15-3-85 + hefty moss*
185ft.   *H. B. Lyon, J. Herbert and H. P. Cain   1923*
An impressive climb for its standard up the big cleft which separates the overhangs of the central mass from the more amenable slabs to the left.
1) 40ft. Easy climbing up the cleft to the belay at the top of pitch 1 of Haste Not. 2) 100ft. Scramble up into the chimney proper and climb this (often wet) with difficulty until a groove out on the left can be gained (arrange protection for the second after this move). Follow the groove to a terrace and block belay. If the chimney is very wet it can be avoided on the left wall. 3) 45ft. Make an awkward diagonal ascent to the right to regain the chimney, and follow this steeply to the top.

91 **White Ghyll Slabs**   *   S
225ft.   *G. Barker and A. T. Hargreaves   1930*
A fine open route on good holds. Start about 25ft. left of

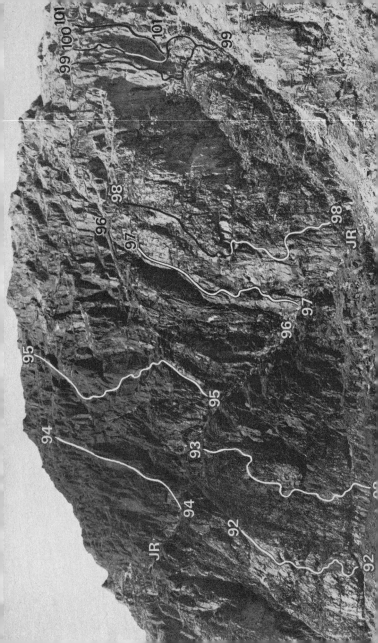

White Ghyll Chimney.

1) 90ft. Good holds lead diagonally leftwards to a ledge below a shallow groove. Go up this to a fine spike belay on the right.   2) 55ft. The steep wall a few feet left of the belay is delicate at first. Better holds then lead rightwards to a terrace and block belay.   3) 80ft. The grooved arete leads to the top of the crag.

PAVEY ARK   (286080)

Situated in a magnificent position overlooking Stickle Tarn, this large cliff rivals Gimmer Crag as the central rock climbing attraction of the Langdale Pikes. It gives a number of climbs between 200 and 300ft. in length and of all standards. Despite its vegetated appearance, most of the climbs are on sound clean rock which is a delight to climb.

Approach: From the New Dungeon Ghyll Hotel, a direct ascent of Mill Ghyll to Stickle Tarn is the obvious approach. From the Old Dungeon Ghyll Hotel it is best to take a traversing path from the Dungeon Ghyll Beck alongside a wall when the Mill Ghyll Path is joined about a third of the way up. Another alternative is the ascent of Middlefell Buttress (q.v.) followed by a traverse of the hillside below the summit crags of Harrison Stickle to reach Stickle Tarn.

Topography and Descents: The cliff is divided into two sections by an oblique series of ledges (Jack's Rake) which runs from the bottom right-hand side of the crag to the top left. Jack's Rake is graded as an easy rock climb, but this does not prevent hordes of tourists from ascending it (and sometimes descending it at speed!) and kicking loose rocks down the crag below. It is therefore even more necessary than usual to wear a helmet and keep an alert look out for falling objects, animal or mineral. The Rake provides a convenient descent from climbs below it or those ending close to the summit. Care should be exercised when descending in wet weather if wearing P.A.'s or similar footwear. Above the foot of the Rake rises Rake End Chimney which makes the left-hand boundary of the third section of the cliff, the East wall, which extends to the right of Rake End Chimney until the cliff fades out in grassy ledges and shallow vegetated chimneys.

Climbs below Jack's Rake
Two gullies to the left, Little Gully and Great Gully (with its great chockstone, well seen from below) provide Moderate and Difficult climbs respectively. To the right of Great Gully rises Stoney Buttress, then a shallow vegetated gully separates this buttress from a sweep of slabs capped by a bulge and curving ledge system, the Crescent.

92 **Crescent Slabs**   **   S
200ft.   *G. S. Bower and A. W. Wakefield 1920*
Start directly below the right-hand end of the Crescent. A fine route on sound compact rock.
1) 80ft. A gangway breaks through the overhang guarding the base of the slabs. Follow the gangway to the left up to a ledge from which an oblique traverse can be made, not without difficulty, into a shallow groove. This too is awkward and is followed by easier slabs to the left up to a spike belay.   2) 35ft. Step right and go up to a thread belay by a large block.   3) 85ft. Climb the block and gain a shallow scoop with difficulty. Step left and go up the delightful slabs to finish at the right-hand end of the Crescent. Jack's Rake lies 100ft. up grassy ledges to the right. The climb can be suitably extended by the ascent of Cook's Tour (q.v.).

93 **Arcturus**   **   HVS
270ft.   *J. A. Austin and E. Metcalf 1963*
To the right of Crescent Slabs the cliff steepens, with a prominent overhang at half height. This wall is defined on the right by a grassy, rightward-slanting break with a holly at its foot. This break is taken by Deception: a vegetated S. The route described here takes the steep slabs and walls to the left. It is a magnificent climb with impressive and varied situations on perfect rock. Start directly below the holly of Deception.
1) 25ft. A slab is climbed to the holly.   2) 95ft. 10ft. left of the holly it is possible to get established on the

39 *On the second pitch of Arcturus, Pavey Ark*

impending wall which protects the slab above. Climb the wall to a foothold on the slab and step left to a piton, or step left below the slab and go up to the piton. Neither way is easy. Climb the slab above bearing slightly left to a good ledge below the overhangs. 3) 105ft. Step right from the ledge and climb a shallow corner, with difficulty at first, to a ledge on the left. Step right and follow a crack to another ledge (good nut runner on the right). Traverse right to a small and very exposed slab. Cross this with difficulty to a good spike, and step down to an excellent ledge and belay. 4) 50ft. The rib above is harder than it appears. Follow it to Jack's Rake. A suitable continuation is Golden Slipper.

Climbs above Jack's Rake

Above Jack's Rake the cliff is less continuous than that below, with large ledges and easier angled rock. Above the finish of Crescent Slabs is Gwynne's Chimney, a good 80ft. D. The first climb starts from Jack's Rake some 20yd. left of Gwynne's Chimney.

94 **Golden Slipper** * HVS
180ft. *J. A. Austin and R. B. Evans 1958*
This aptly named route takes the front of the slender pillar to the left of Gwynne's Chimney. The delightful second pitch, on perfect rock, is remarkable for its lack of protection. 1) 40ft. A short wall guards the foot of the pillar. Follow a gangway up to the right to a small ledge. A series of strenuous layback moves leads to the ledges below the pillar. 2) 80ft. Climb the steepening slab on small holds to a nut runner where the slab approaches wall angle. Move right and up to a ledge and belay. A sustained pitch. 3) 60ft. The rib on the left to the top.

95 **Cook's Tour** * VD
295ft. *J. W. Cook and G. B. Elliot 1943*
A devious route on good rock. It takes the easiest break midway between Rake End Chimney and Gwynne's Chimney, a leftwards-facing chimney-crack. Harder in wet conditions. 1) 20ft. The open groove to a good belay. 2) 30ft. The steep slab above is followed by a traverse right to a large pinnacle. 3) 45ft. Easy climbing on the left leads to ledges

below the rectangular slab. 4) 75ft. Traverse left along ledges to a flake belay. 5) 20ft. Climb a shallow gully and move right to a grass ledge and pinnacle belay.
6) 40ft. Traverse right and up to a corner with an ash, then follow the crack behind the tree to a belay up on the left. 7) 60ft. The slab above is climbed to a stance (but poor belay), and the wall above gives good holds for the ascent to the top.

96 **Rake End Chimney** ** D
165ft. *G. W. Barton 1898*
A fine climb on good rock. The obvious chimney above the foot of Jack's Rake gives an all-weather climb of continuous interest.
1) 100ft. (Can be split). The chimney is followed over several chockstones to a large ledge. Good belay at the point of arrival. Walk up to another belay in a cave.
2) 65ft. Climb onto a large chockstone at the back of the cave. Pass through an opening onto the right wall. A small cave is passed on the left to the top.

THE EAST WALL

This formidable wall gives the finest climbs on the crag. The climbs are in two groups, those on the area immediately to the right of Rake End Chimney, and those on the East Wall proper: the steep wall overlooking the scree gully running up to the right from the foot of Jake's Rake. Descent from all these climbs, including Rake End Chimney, is best made by traversing well to the right, and descending the tourist route for about 30yds., when the top of the scree gully can be gained by the descent of a short but awkward chockstone pitch.

Rake End Wall ** VS
97 210ft. *H. A. Carsten and E. Phillips 1945*
This magnificent climb takes the steep pillar immediately right of Rake End Chimney. It is a sustained climb with varied technique, good protection and perfect rock.
Start 15ft. right of Rake End Chimney.
1) 70ft. Climb the steep wall past a prominent flake until it is necessary to make a traverse to the right to a stance on the right of a large block. 2) 35ft. Mount the block and go

up the overhanging crack above. A hidden side-hold on the left wall is of material assistance. Thread belay on the right.   3) 65ft. From the lower left-hand end of the ledge step left to gain the foot of the steep slab. Climb the slab into a small groove on the right of a small overhang. After a few feet quit the groove on the left and climb the arete to the large terrace.   4) 40ft. Walk up to the next section of the wall. Climb the arete on the right of the last pitch of Rake End Chimney to the top.

98   **Stoats' Crack**   **   HS
345ft.   *B. R. Record and J. R. Jenkins   1933*
Above the point where Jack's Rake runs into the ground, a subsidiary buttress lies against the main mass of the crag. The crack thus formed on the right provides the initial pitch of this varied climb.
1) 25ft. Climb a wet groove to the foot of the crack.   2) 30ft. Scramble up to a terrace at the foot of the crack proper.
3) 25ft. Walk left to the foot of the crack.   4) 65ft. The crack is followed until good holds on the left wall give access to a ledge and belay.   5) 85ft. Traverse left into a groove and climb this, not without interest, to an overhung ledge.
6) 80ft. Move left along the terrace and climb an open groove to another ledge. Move left along this to an easy groove which leads back rightwards to a ledge and small belay.   7) 90ft. Climb the slabs on the right of the belay, first straight up, then bearing left to the top.

99   **Astra**   ***   XS
295ft.   *E. Metcalf and J. A. Austin   1960*
A superb slab climb on good rock with magnificent situations. About halfway up the scree gully to the right of Stoats' Crack a conspicuous slab slanting right, forming the right wall of a huge open corner, will be seen. Start almost directly below this at a small break giving access to an area of less steep slabs.
1) 60ft. Gain the slabs and make an ascending traverse left to a grassy terrace and collapsing tree.   2) 35ft. The wall above leads into the corner and the start of the difficulties.   3) 70ft. Traverse right below the steep wall to the arete (runner in a thin crack just to the left). Move round the arete with difficulty onto the slab where the angle eases but the holds diminish alarmingly. Move across the slab to a flake which provides a welcome respite. This is

left reluctantly for the uncertain security of a sloping ledge some 15ft. higher to the left. The short wall on the right is crossed with the aid of a piton and a stance reached immediately. Piton belay.   4) 115ft. Continue up the slab above to a ledge below a V-groove. This is often wet and always awkward. Climb it to a ledge and belay.   5) 15ft. The crack above.

100 **Fallen Angel** ** XS
26oft.   *E. Grindley and I. Roper   1972*
This very hard climb takes the slanting overhanging groove immediately right of Astra. A fine natural line. Start at the same point as Astra.

1) 8oft. Gain the slabs and go up the right edge, overlooking the gully, to a grass ledge. Move left and up a short corner to a rock ledge and belays.   2) 75ft. Traverse left to the groove and climb this until it slants up to the right. Continue up the groove with great difficulty (two pegs in place) until the groove opens out. Transfer onto a slab on the right and climb this on small holds to a good foothold and piton belay. A very sustained pitch.   3) 8oft. Climb the thin crack above for 2oft. and step right to gain another crack slanting right to a pedestal on the arete. Step left into a V-groove and climb this on small holds, passing an awkward overhang, to a ledge and belay.   4) 25ft. The slab above leads to the top.

101 **Cascade** ** HVS
23oft.   *J. A. Austin and R. B. Evans   1957*
Another fine climb taking the last clean, rightward-slanting slab on the crag. Like the other routes on this wall it gives sustained and interesting climbing on sound compact rock. Small runners only protect the crux. Start at the same point as Astra and Fallen Angel.

1) 8oft. As for Fallen Angel.   2) 6oft. The steepening slab on the right is climbed with increasing difficulty. After 4oft. a series of difficult bridging moves in the corner leads to a loose spike 5ft. below a grass ledge at the top of the slab. Move right to gain a stance and belay.   3) 9oft. The short wall above the point of arrival is climbed to the foot of a prominent chimney. Climb this and continue in the same line to the top of the crag.

103

GIMMER CRAG (273030)

This imposing buttress is one of the finest and most popular cliffs in the Lake District, with a wide range of climbs of all standards, except the easiest, on rock that is nearly always perfect. The cliff has a southerly aspect and dries quickly after rain.

Approaches: From the New Dungeon Ghyll Hotel the Dungeon Ghyll path is followed up the left bank of the Dungeon Ghyll stream. After a series of zigzags the path emerges on a plateau below the cliffs of Harrison Stickle. Gimmer Crag's south-east face is visible to the left, recognisable by the narrow cleft of Gimmer Chimney. After crossing the plateau the path starts to rise and swing away to the right. At this point a level trod, indefinite at first, branches left, crossing a small beck on route, to the foot of the south-east face. 1¼ hours. The Old Dungeon Ghyll Hotel is the more usual starting point. The path from the New Hotel can be gained by a steep ascent of the scree gully slightly east of the Old Hotel, or by the ascent of Middlefell Buttress (q.v.) and the steep hillside above. A third alternative is to follow a path which goes up the hillside just west of Middlefell Buttress, directly above Middlefell Farm. At the top of a wall on the left a scree chute is entered and ascended until the path breaks out onto the hillside above. It then leads a good deal more pleasantly to the crag. It is usual to go to the crag by one of the other routes and descend by the last. Time in ascent 1¼– 1½ hours.

Topography and Descents: The cliff has three faces, South-east, West and North-west, the division being two rather indefinite aretes. The main cliff is separated from the hillside by two deep-cut gullies, South-east, obvious from the point of arrival, and Junipall, which cleaves the North-west face and separates it from Pallid Buttress. Both gullies provide convenient descents, although a rope should be used by parties of limited experience, and care should be exercised to avoid knocking down loose stones as there may be more than one party in the gully at the same time.

The climbs on the South-east Face start at the point of arrival, while those on the West Face commence from a terrace (Ash Tree Ledge) some distance up the cliff. This

40 Cascade, Pavey Ark, moving right at the top of pitch 2

terrace is reached by a well-scratched scramble which commences at the end of a small terrace which cuts into the cliff at the point of arrival. A short flaky rib (the Bilberry Chute) gives access to a long terrace above which a series of ledges and short walls gives access to Ash Tree Ledge. The North-west Face can be reached by climbing the Bilberry Chute to the first terrace. This is crossed to its left end, and an easy traverse followed to the top of a 30ft. chimney which is descended with some difficulty into North-west Gully. A much easier alternative is to walk round the toe of the buttress and scramble up North-west Gully.

102 **Gimmer Chimney** * VD
260ft.   *E. Rigby, J. Sanderson and A. S. Thompson   1902*
The long crack bisecting the South-east Face gives a climb of sustained interest. Start directly below the crack line.
1) 45ft. Climb a broken rib to a stance and belays.
2) 25ft. Continue up an easy chimney to a grass ledge and good belay.   3) 30ft. Easy rocks are climbed, after an awkward move, to a good stance on the right.   4) 55ft. Move left into a groove. This is difficult and leads to a sentry box with a small spike runner. The deep crack above is followed to a large stance below twin chimneys.
5) 35ft. Move right and climb the right-hand chimney into an open gully. Good belay.   6) 70ft. A few feet in the gully bed, followed by an ascent of the right-hand rib, leads to the top.

103 **Bracket and Slab Climb** * HS
295ft.   *H. B. Lyon and J. Herbert   1923*
A varied climb taking a parallel line to Gimmer Chimney, including the chimney to the left of pitch 5 of that climb. The omission of this chimney renders the climb a good deal easier. Start at a flake belay 20ft. above the point where the path meets the crag.
1) 35ft. Step off the top of the flake and go up an awkward slab to a bilberry ledge.   2) 65ft. Traverse right to gain a rib which is followed to a grassy rake. Go up this to a rocky corner at the top.   3) 40ft. The Bracket. On the

41 *Gimmer Crag, S.E. Face*
A = Ash Tree Lodge   B = Approach via Bilberry Chute
C = Amen Corner   D = Descent via S.E. Gully

right a series of blocks project from the wall. These are traversed to gain an awkward groove. Go up this to a belay at its top. 4) 40ft. Diagonally right over easy rocks to a small belay at the foot of a steep wall. It is probably better to fix a runner and press on. 5) 25ft. The Neat Bit. A footledge leads diagonally leftwards to the foot of a short crack. This leads to a slab below an impending wall. 6) 25ft. Walk 25ft. right to a belay at the foot of a smooth chimney. Climb this appallingly smooth and strenuous cleft to a belay in the gully above. (Those who avoid it for the easier one of Gimmer Chimney 15ft. to the right will be forgiven). 7) 65ft. Work leftwards then back to the right, up pleasant slabs to the top.

THE WEST FACE

As mentioned earlier, the climbs on this face start from Ash Tree Ledge. A complex network of routes exists on the right-hand side of the face, of VD-HS in standard. In general the routes take shallow groove lines connected by short traverses. Most of the lines are indistinct, however, and often difficult to follow, so only one route is described on this section of the crag.

104 **'B' Route** ** MS

18oft. *H. B. Lyon, J. Stables and A. S. Thompson 1907*
This interesting route takes a line close to the right-hand edge of the West Face. Start at the right-hand end of Ash Tree Ledge. 'A', 'B' and 'C' routes are arrowed and have a common start up a line of cracked blocks.

1) 30ft. Diagonally right over the blocks to a large platform 2) 15ft. Move right to a short crack which leads to another platform (Thompson's Ledge). On the right is a belay at the foot of Amen Corner. 3) 15ft. The crack in the corner is strenuous but short and safe with a well-used landing platform below. Emerge on the gangway and belay on the left. 4) 70ft. The gangway curves up to the left to the foot of Green Chimney (a misnomer if ever there was one: it is an open groove). Follow the chimney until it is possible to cross the right wall to a finely-situated ledge— the Crow's Nest. 5) 50ft. Step right and ascend pleasant slabs to the top.

The next three climbs on the West Face are described in

conjunction with routes on the lower section of the North-west Face, since in combination they give sustained climbs of respectable length. Kipling Groove, 'F' and 'D' Routes can be started from Ash Tree Ledge.

105 **Ash Tree Slabs/'D' Route** ** HVD/S
255ft.   *G. S. Bower and A. W. Wakefield 1920*
G. S. Bower and P. R. Masson 1919
A pleasant combination of slabs and a good crack. The route starts on the North-West Face of the lower buttress up slabs on the left wall of a prominent corner, some 50ft. above a huge detached flake.
1) 50ft. Move up the corner then traverse left on good holds to the edge. Follow this to a good ledge and belay.
2) 55ft. Move up left to a large ledge, then climb a groove leading up to the right.   3) 50ft. Continue up to the left to a ledge mid-way between Ash Tree Ledge and an overhanging, triangular recess marking the start of the crack line of 'D' Route.   4) 40ft. Climb a groove to enter the recess, then make a delicate traverse left for 15ft. Follow a groove back right to a good stance and block belay.
5) 45ft. Climb the 'Forked Lightning Crack' to belays on the left wall.   6) 15ft. Move up to a sloping corner on the left, when a delicate balance move leads to the finishing holds.

106 **Intern/Kipling Groove** *** HVS
330ft.   *P. Fearnehough, G. Oliver and J. Hesmondhalgh 1963*
A. R. Dolphin and J. B. Lockwood 1948
Although these two climbs make a good combination, Kipling Groove is of course an excellent climb in its own right and can be started from Ash Tree Ledge (at the left-hand end, 50ft. below the large overhangs). Intern starts on the lower buttress some 20ft. left of Ash Tree Slabs at an overhanging groove.
1) 60ft. The groove slants up to the right and is awkward. From a small stance at its top swing down to the left onto a leftward-slanting slab. Follow this up to the left, using holds over the bulge (when they appear!) into a bulging corner. Move up this onto a sloping ledge on the left, when another easier corner leads to a stance with a belay up to the left.
2) 55ft. From the belay spike step right onto the steep wall and go up this over an awkward overhang into a groove

which is followed without difficulty to a small stance and belay.   3) 40ft. Step left onto the arete and go up this, using a thin flake crack in the last few feet, to Ash Tree Ledge, and the start of Kipling Groove.   4) 40ft. Climb the wall at the left-hand end of the ledge to a small belay but good stance below the overhangs.   5) 35ft. Move up to the overhangs and traverse left using the undercut crack, with difficulty at first, to the foot of a thin crack. Go up this to a stance at the foot of the overhanging groove. 6) 100ft. A superb pitch. Climb the groove passing a dubious block with care until forced onto the arete on the right. Climb the thin crack until it is necessary to step right again below a bulge. This is split by a crack running up to the right. A strenuous traverse is made along this crack for 15ft. to a welcome resting place below a narrow crack which leads, still with some difficulty, to the top of the crag.

107   **North West Arete/'F' Route**   **   VS
295ft.   *R. J. Birkett and V. Veevers   1940/1941*
The start of this route lies some 20ft. left of Intern at a grassy slab sloping up to the left. This route provides an interesting contrast, with the open wall and rib climbing of its lower half, and the strenuous crack in its upper section. 1) 30ft. Climb up to the slab and follow it up to the left to a flake belay.   2) 135ft. Step right onto the steep wall and climb it for a few feet until it is possible to traverse right again to a short crack leading up to an overhang. The overhang is split by a short groove on the left. This is climbed strenuously to a good spike, and excellent holds are then followed diagonally rightwards to an airy rib. Follow the rib, with a short diversion to the right, until a short crack leads to Ash Tree Ledge.   3) 25ft. Scramble up to the right to belay directly below the huge corner line of 'F' route.   4) 35ft. Move up to a small ledge then climb a bulge on the left to reach a small stance and belay below the overhangs.   5) 70ft. A fine, strenuous pitch. Move up right and climb the corner with increasing difficulty to the top of the crag.

42 Pitch 2 of Kipling Groove, Gimmer Crag

108 Gimmer String   **   XS

250ft.   *J. A. Austin, D. Miller and E. Metcalf   1963*

This magnificent climb takes the arete separating the
North-west and West Faces. Fine positions and good
protection make it the most popular climb of its standard
in the area. Start at the foot of Gimmer Crack, the obvious
corner crack running up the right-hand side of the face.
1) 110ft. Climb the corner crack to a small ledge then
traverse left into a groove. Follow this more easily to an
area of ledges. Above on the right is a monolith below a
large overhang. Scramble up to a stance just beneath this.
2) 60ft. Climb the monolith and step right to the foot of a
wide crack. This is followed, not without difficulty for
those of more than average girth, to the stance below the
groove of Kipling Groove.   3) 80ft. Bridge up the groove
until good holds permit a short hand traverse to a niche
on the arete. A steep shallow groove is climbed with
difficulty until a move left can be made onto the wall
overlooking Gimmer Crack. Good holds then give a
pleasant interlude before the final wall is reached. This is
climbed by precarious bridging moves (crux) to reach
ledges at the top of the crag.

109 Gimmer Crack   *   MVS**

240ft.   *A. B. Reynolds and G. G. MacPhee   1928*

A superb natural line up the obvious corner at the right-hand
side of the North-West Face. One of the best climbs of its
standard in the District. Starts at the same point as Gimmer
String at the foot of a narrow corner crack.
1) 85ft. Scramble up to the crack and follow it to a small
ledge. Cross the wall on the left with difficulty, keeping as
low as possible, to a ledge below a shallow groove which is
climbed on improving holds to a pedestal belay. 2) 25ft.
The pedestal provides the take-off for a fierce little
mantelshelf. Follow a sloping ledge up to the left to a good
stance and belay. 3) 45ft. After a strenuous move, follow
the arete above until it is possible to traverse back right
into the crack.   4) 15ft. The Sentry Box is climbed onto the
Bower, a fine gathering point from which to view the
antics of the leader on the next pitch. 5) 70ft. Go straight
up the crack to a small overhang which is only overcome

43 North West Arete, Gimmer Crag

with considerable expenditure of energy. A small ledge
provides a welcome resting place before the ascent of the
final awkward chimney.

110 **Hiatus**   *   VS
325ft.   *G. S. Bower, A. B. Reynolds, A. W. Wakefield
and G. G. MacPhee   1927*
The climb follows grassy slabs on the left of the Crack,
and turns the huge overhangs by a long traverse left. The
situations improve as height is gained. Start 6ft. left of
Gimmer Crack.
1) 40ft. A steep wall leads to a terrace. Traverse up and
left to a corner and belay.   2) 35ft. An awkward scoop on
the right is followed by a ridge to the pedestal belay on the
Crack.   3) 30ft. Move across to a mantelshelf on the left.
Follow the slab to a grass ledge.   4) 55ft. A grassy gully for
30ft. followed by a traverse left.   5) 50ft. Another terrace
leads back to the gully. Move up and traverse left across a
mossy wall to ledges and belays.   6) 70ft. Move up into
a corner then step across a large block and make a delicate
tracerse left up the slab below overhangs. Climb a steep
corner for 10ft. then continue the traverse to the second
of two ribs. Climb this to a good niche and belay.   7) 45ft.
The slab on the left is followed by an awkward groove.
Grooves Traverse Finish: A very fine alternative.
6b) 55ft. Move up into the corner then traverse right
across the steep wall to gain a groove. Follow this to a small
stance and good belay.   7b) 55ft. Climb the mossy groove
for 10ft. then traverse delicately right for 15ft. below a
small overhang. Continue up right on good holds to the top.

RAVEN CRAG   (285065)

This easily accessible crag can be reached in 15 minutes
steep ascent from the Old Dungeon Ghyll Hotel, and in a
slightly longer time from the New Hotel. It is useful as a
quick-drying alternative to the higher crags in inclement
weather, or for an evening or half day, although none of
the routes compete in quality with those already described
elsewhere. The rock is in general clean and sound, and
the climbing rarely serious in nature.

44   *Gimmer Crag, N.W. Face   A = Ash Tree Ledge*

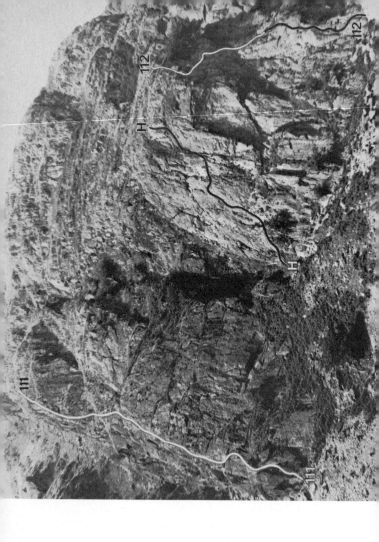

45 Raven Crag, Great Langdale
    H = Holly Tree Traverse (VD)

Middlefell Buttress   *   D (first pitch S but can be avoided)

250ft.   *J. Laycock, S. W. Herford and A. R. Thompson*   *1911*

Hundreds of beginners must have taken their first steps on rock on this climb. The route lies on the clean left-hand buttress of Raven Crag, directly above the left-hand boundary of the enclosure. (The climb is a useful approach to Gimmer Crag or Pavey Ark). The climb starts at a steep crack at the toe of the buttress.

1) 50ft. The crack has been polished to a high gloss by myriads of sweating palms and flailing boots, and proves strenuous. A platform is reached at 40ft. and a higher ledge reached without further difficulty. Easier alternatives lie to left or right, or the pitch may be avoided entirely.
2) 30ft. A polished slab at the back of ledge is climbed by a variety of routes. Good belays.   3) 120ft. A groove in the nose of the buttress is entered with some difficulty from either left or right. Big holds then lead to a large boulder on another platform. Stances and belays *en route* as required.
3) 50ft. The steep wall above is quite difficult, a small overhang being surmounted by traversing in from either left or right. Descend via the gully on the left.

Bilberry Buttress   VS

255ft.   *C. F. Rolland and J. F. Renwich*   *1941*

Although artificial in its line, this route gives a sustained series of crack pitches unusual in Langdale. The main buttress of Raven Crag is guarded by large overhangs in the centre. Just right of these a ridge projects downwards, separating the south and east faces of the buttress. Start at the lowest point of the right-hand side of the crag.

1) 25ft. Easy climbing leads to the foot of the first crack.
2) 40ft. Climb the crack by fist jams to gain an open scoop. Follow this up to the left to a ledge and flake belays.
3) 55ft. The steep wall above is capped by a bulge, and split by a thin crack. Step right off the belay flake into the crack and climb this with difficulty to a hidden jug. Easier climbing up the arete on the left leads to a long shattered ledge. Thread belay at point of arrival.   4) 40ft. Move along to the right to the foot of the first feasible looking crack in the wall above. Climb this on widely spaced holds to a stance behind a large block.   5) 50ft. Climb down to the left of the block until it is possible to traverse left in

an exposed position below a line of overhangs into a recess.
Move left from the recess to gain easy ground and the top
of the crag.
Descent is best made by following an airy path to the
right (east) until a short descent over some split blocks
gives access to a ledge (Oak Tree Terrace) which slants
down to the foot of the crag.

BOWFELL   (245069)

Approach: This cliff lies just north of the summit of Bowfell
and faces east. It is reached by the ascent of the Band
to where the tourist path bears left. Continue straight
ahead here, then bear right to reach the start of a horizontal
track (the Climbers' Traverse) which leads along below
Flat Crags to a spring at the foot of the Cambridge Crag.
Cross a scree chute to the foot of Bowfell Buttress.
Descent: Down the scree gully on the left (south).

113   **Bowfell Buttress**   ***   VD
305ft.   *T. Shaw, L. J. Oppenheimer and party*   1902
This well-polished classic takes the general line of the nose
of the buttress and starts just left of the lowest point of
the crag. On the left of the Buttress is a broad scree fan then
a steep crag with three prominent grooves. The following route
takes the right-hand and largest groove.
1) 45ft. Up the ridge to a good belay.   2) 30ft. The
smooth chimney on the right is not without interest.
Continue more easily to a terrace.   3) 40ft. Climb
diagonally left to a sentry box.   4) 6oft. Climb the
chimney above for 40ft. to a good belay. Easy ledges then
lead to a broad platform. Go down this to the right to a
belay below a steep crack.   5) 55ft. Climb the crack
(smooth and awkward) then slabby rocks (crux in winter)
sloping leftwards to a pinnacle.   6) 40ft. Move left and up
a slanting groove to a chimney and follow this to a flake
belay.   7) 20ft. The wall above followed by a move left
to a belay of impressive proportions.   8) 6oft. Step back
right and continue up the groove to the top.

113A   **Sword of Damocles**   **   XS
180ft.   *A. R. Dolphin, P. J. Greenwood and D. Hopkin*   1952

46 Bowfell Buttress

A splendid climb, with good situations to compensate for its brevity. Starts from a grass ledge below and just left of the large groove and beneath a prominent curved crack.

1) 30ft. Traverse up and right along the curved crack to a groove, which leads to a stance and belay behind a large pinnacle. 2) 30ft. Climb the groove on the right until a long step right can be made to a ledge and belay on the ledge. 3) 60ft. Go up until it is possible to traverse across the groove to the left wall. Continue up the groove to a large detached flake (the Sword) which is used for progress. Continue with difficulty until a move right leads to easier rock and a stance and belay. 4) 60ft. Climb the steep and impressive flake-crack above to the summit.

NECKBAND CRAG (261062)

Approach: This small cliff (Earing Crag on the OS map) lies due north of the summit of the Band and is reached by following the path as for Bowfell Buttress (qv) until the col just beyond the summit of the Band is reached. The crag lies to the north-east of the col and is reached by descending until it is possible to contour below broken crags.

The principal features of the crag are three great corners split by equally fine aretes. The four climbs described are all of great character and are on superb rock, which is unfortunately rather mossy, and therefore slow to dry.

Descent: The climbs finish on a terrace above which another 100ft. or so of climbing can be constructed. It is however without interest and it is normal practice to traverse left to descend well to the left of the crag.

113B **Cravat** * VS
120ft. *H. Drasdo and N. Drasdo 1950*
The climb lies at the extreme left-hand end of the crag and starts at the foot of the short grassy corner. It is steep and not too well protected.

1) 120ft. Climb the corner to a grass ledge then step right and climb a thin crack by long reaches until a line of holds leads out right to a niche on the arete. Continue the upward traverse round the arete and so into the big groove on the right which leads on good holds to the top.

113C **Gandalf's Groove** ** Mild XS

47 *Deer Bield Crag, Far Easedale*

115ft. *J. A. Austin and F. P. Jenkinson 1964*
This good climb takes the first big corner to the right of Cravat,
and gives difficulties both strenuous and delicate.

1) 115ft. Climb the corner over a series of bulges until, at 55ft.,
a descending traverse leads to the left-hand rib. Climb the
delicate wall just right of this until a final hard move can be
made on to the rib itself. (Junction with Cravat). Either follow
Cravat to finish up the corner, or after a few feet continue up
the slabby wall just right of the arete. Variation: instead of
traversing left to the arete at 55ft., continue directly up the
corner. More strenuous but well worthwhile.

113D **Gillette** * XS
115ft. *K. Wood and J. A. Austin 1968*
This climb should appeal to the technician, requiring finesse
rather than strong-arm tactics. The climb starts about 20ft.
right of Gandalf's Groove at an impending flake crack.

1) 115ft. Climb the crack to the overhang (good thread) then
step left and climb the long, thin gangway overlooking
Gandalf's Groove. Difficulties are continuous to the finishing
'jug'.

113E **Razor Crack** XS
120ft. *J. A. Austin and K. Wood 1966*
The fourth route described adds yet another dimension to the
climbing on this crag. The wall crack on the right-hand side of
the arete taken by Gillette gives a strenuous and sustained
route. Start as for Gillette.

1) 120ft. Climb the crack to the overhang, then traverse right
and pull over the overhang into the main crack. This is followed
past another overhang at 75ft. after which difficulties ease
somewhat.

DEER BIELD CRAG (303087)
The crag is small but very steep, with smooth rock that
gives either enormous jugs or nothing at all; thus the
climbing in general is strenuous. The central buttress of
the crag is completely detached, forming a fissure on either
side, Deer Bield Crack on the left and Deer Bield Chimney
on the right. The latter is a loose S and is not recommended.
Approach: This cliff does not lie in Langdale at all, but in

48 Over the first crux on Deer Bield Buttress

the lonely valley of Far Easedale above Grasmere. The best approach is from Grasmere up the Greenup Edge path. The cliff is the only one of any size on the left-hand side of the valley (1 hour). Alternatively from Langdale ascend Mill Ghyll to Stickle Tarn then strike north-eastward passing above Easedale Tarn to the top of the crag (1½ hours).

Descent: Best made round the left (SE) side of the buttress.

Deer Bield Crack   ***   HVS

114

170ft.   *A. T. Hargreaves and G. G. MacPhee*   *1930*

A remarkable climb for its antiquity! This is not a climb to be taken lightly as strong parties have been known to fail. Start at a prominent flake 15ft. left of the lowest point of the buttress.

1) 35ft. The crack above the flake is soon quitted for a niche on the right. Continue up the crack to a recess. The slab on the left is then climbed on good holds to a ledge on the right wall. Thread belay.   2) 25ft. The chimney on the left to a large block belay.   3) 20ft. Continue up a shallow chimney, passing some loose blocks with care, to a belay in a pear-shaped chimney.   4) 35ft. A very strenuous pitch! Climb the chimney facing right, and as deeply inside as possible, to a chockstone runner in the roof. Traverse right below the roof and continue to a resting place and chockstone belay.   5) 40ft. The narrower crack above eases after 10ft., and leads to a belay below a super-Amen Corner.   6) 15ft. Summoning all reserves of energy (and, if *in extremis*, the second man's shoulders too!) climb the corner.

Deer Bield Buttress   ***   XS

115

185ft.   *A. R. Dolphin and A. D. Brown*   *1951*

This very good climb takes a groove line immediately to the right of Deer Bield Crack, and provides difficulties of both strenuous and delicate nature maintained at a high standard. Start at the lowest point of the crag.

1) 45ft. A layback crack slants up to the left to join Deer Bield Crack. Follow it to a recess below an impending crack.   2) 15ft. The crack is climbed on fist jams to the belay at the end of pitch 1 of Deer Bield Crack.   3) 35ft. The first crux. Step right from the stance and make a difficult layback move to gain a tiny ledge on the wall.

Move up with even more difficulty to a resting place and good nut runner. A very steep crack then leads to a stance below a long groove. 4) 90ft. Climb the groove to a small overhang, above which the groove forks. Pass the overhang with difficulty to gain the right-hand groove and follow this until it is necessary to move delicately right to a scoop. Climb up left to a pinnacle (poor stance) and from this traverse left on very small holds to a thin flake crack (second crux). The crack is climbed by layback to easy ground.

WINTER CLIMBING

This low-lying, sunny valley is not noted for good snow and ice climbing! Bowfell is the most popular area, where the gullies near Bowfell Buttress provide interesting Grade I climbs, and the Buttress itself is much more serious. With a covering of snow and ice it is generally Grade III. Elsewhere in Langdale, good conditions in winter are very rare. The gullies and Jack's Rake on Pavey Ark have provided good sport, although the crag does catch the sun. The nearest reliable winter climbing is on Great End, which is reached in about two hours after the ascent of Rossett Ghyll. See Borrowdale section.

PATTERDALE AREA

Often described as the most scenic valley in the Lake District, the area around Patterdale is also the most crowded, especially in the summer months. Patterdale is the centre for climbing in Grisedale, Deepdale and Dovedale. The crags in these three valleys are usually approached from the east, and offer a good variety of climbing. None of the crags is near the road; the nearest (Eagle Crag, Grisedale) is reached in about 30 minutes. The crags are shown on the Thirlmere map.

Access

From the M6, via the Penrith junction and the A592 through Pooley Bridge. From the south, via Kirkstone Pass from Ambleside or Troutbeck. The nearest railway station is at Penrith, and there is a bus service between Penrith and Patterdale. There are also Mountain Goat minibus services from Bowness and Ambleside.

Accommodation and Camping

There is a campsite near the Brothers Water Hotel, ½ mile south of the lake (401119), and also at Glenridding (380167). Hotels and guest houses are found in Patterdale, Glenridding, Low Hartsop, and at the south end of Brothers Water and the summit of the Kirkstone Pass. There is a Youth Hostel at Patterdale (399156) and one at Glenridding (366173). Elsewhere there is an Outward Bound School (438212) and a Sheffield University Club Hut (355135) in Grisedale.

Food and Drink

There are several excellent restaurants in the hotels mentioned above, and cafés in Glenridding and Patterdale. Typically, the café in Patterdale opens from Easter until the end of September. Most of the hotels have bars, the most popular with climbers being the White Lion at Patterdale or the Brothers Water Hotel south of the tarn. Normal licensing hours are 11–3, 5.30–10.30, S. 12–2, 7–10.30. Shops and PO at Patterdale and Glenridding, EC Fri.

Garages and Car Hire

Petrol, repairs, and car hire at Scafoot Garage (tel. Glenridding 334) closing time 8.30 p.m. in summer, 7.00 p.m. in winter. Taxi Glenridding 215. Nearest AA garage with 24 hour breakdown service is in Ambleside, tel. 3273.

There is a tourist information office at the Brothers Water campsite in the summer. Telephones at Patterdale and the north end of Brothers Water (Low Hartsop junction). Public toilets at Patterdale. The nearest equipment shops are in Ambleside (10 miles) or Keswick (17 miles).

Mountain Rescue

For assistance, ring first the local POLICE (999). There are manned rescue posts at the Patterdale Hotel (394160, tel. Glenridding 231) and at the Ullswater O.B. School (438213, tel. Pooley Bridge 347). There is a first aid post at the YH in Glenridding (366174, tel. Glenridding 269), and an unmanned post by the wall at the foot of Striding Edge (359155).

EAGLE CRAG, GRISEDALE   (357143)

Although there are in fact two sections to Eagle Crag the routes described are all on the south (left-hand) crag.

The crags look very broken from below but the routes are all much better than they appear. The rock is good and gives incut holds, but the crag is rather lichenous and is slippery in wet conditions. The routes are generally well-protected.

Approach: From the bridge ½ mile north of Patterdale, it is possible to drive about 1 mile up Grisedale. Then follow the track up the valley eventually crossing the stream below Eagle Crag, which is approached directly. About 30 minutes in all.

Descent: Easily down the left-hand (west) side of the crag.

116 **Kestrel Wall**   HS

165ft.   *R. J. Birkett and A. H. Griffin   1954*

A good steep climb on good holds. Start about 30ft. left of the 40ft. slab at the foot of the West Buttress: there are two cracks directly above.

1) 25ft. Climb to the rock ledge. Nut belays.   2) 50ft. Climb the left-hand crack, moving left at the top to belay behind a large perched block.   3) 30ft. The wall above to the large grass ledge.   4) 20ft. A steep slab, on the right, to the upper ledge.   5) 40ft. Pull into a groove above the

49 *Eagle Crag, Grisedale*

right-hand end of the ledge. Move up then step right and finish up a fine rib.

117 **Sobrenada** * VS
205ft. *M. A. James, G. A. Leaver and K. A. Brookes* 1957
An excellent and well-protected climb which is much better than it looks. Start up a 40ft. slab at the foot of the West Buttress.
1) 45ft. Climb the slab direct to a stance and belay.
2) 80ft. Move right and pull up into the cave. Pull out left into a short corner. Climb this, then step right and ascend a wall followed by a rib to a large grass ledge and block belay. 3) 80ft. From a point just right of the blocks traverse right and upwards for 20ft. then go up 10ft. Make an awkward traverse left into a corner which is climbed onto a slab, the exit being even more awkward. Move left then gain a higher slab which is followed to the top.

118 **Doctor's Grooves** HS
235ft. *F. Fitzgerald and G. A. Leaver* 1956
Quite a long climb with a mountaineering atmosphere and plenty of variety. Start just right of the toe of the buttress at the right-hand end of the crag.
1) 40ft. Pull up left onto a slab, then climb up and right to belay on an ash tree. 2) 50ft. Ascend the steep corner above to a grass ledge. 3) 30ft. Move up grass ledges on the left into a corner. 4) 30ft. Traverse the steep wall on the right, then climb straight up to grassy ledges. Scramble up 60ft. to a large block belay at the foot of a steep groove.
5) 65ft. Climb the rib on the right of the groove, then cross the groove to the arete on its left. Pull onto a slab; traverse across to a corner which leads to a ledge and belay.
6) 20ft. A fine steep chimney-crack to finish.

HUTAPLE CRAG (367120)
The long valley of Deepdale cuts deeply into the Fairfield Massif. At its head are two combes, Sleet Cove and Link Cove, to the north and south respectively of the spur of Greenhow End. Hutaple Crag, a big, rather grassy cliff, occupies a commanding position in Sleet Cove facing St. Sunday Crag. The crag gives long mountaineering routes, but dries slowly after rain.

Approach: Directly up Deepdale, bearing right into Sleet
Cove. Scramble up to the foot of the crag on the left
(2 hours).

Topography: The cliff is bounded by East and West Hutaple
Gullies, and a shallow gully splits the face of the crag itself
(Curving Gully, VD). The two climbs described below are
both based on the big recess or corner to the left of
Curving Gully.

Descent: To the right, cross the grassy funnel above West
Hutaple Gully and descend a grassy groove to the west of
the rock ribs which bound the West Gully.

119 **The Amphitheatre** * VS

325ft. *A. D. Marsden and G. Batty 1955*

Start directly below the big corner at the left-hand side of a
triangle of grassy slabs.

1) 85ft. The slab is climbed until it is necessary to move
right to a shallow groove. Go up this to a ledge and cross
this to a broken groove on the right.   2) 90ft. A fine pitch.
Climb up the wall to the right of the groove. Move left
then up to the right onto a slab. A delicate move is made
up to the right and an obvious line taken through the
overhangs to a stance and piton belay.   3) 70ft. Step left
into a steep corner, and follow this to a long terrace.
Move right to the right-hand side of the prominent
buttress.   4) 80ft. Move up into a niche then traverse left
and climb the buttress to easy ground. Scramble up to
cairned ledges. Descent is down a rake into the wide gully
to the right of the crag.

120 **Sleet Wall** S

330ft. *J. C. Duckworth and G. Batty 1952*

A clean, sound route of continuous interest. Start about
30ft. left of the Amphitheatre at a gangway above 30ft. of
scrambling.

1) 35ft. Follow the gangway and move back left to a small
stance.   2) 25ft. Move left then slant rightwards to an
overhung ledge.   3) 65ft. Traverse right and follow the
impressive line back leftwards to a big ledge.   4) 30ft.
Above are two cracks. The right-hand one is followed to a
grassy corner.   5) 35ft. Traverse right and up round the
rib. Easier climbing then follows to a grass ledge.   6) 90ft.
Scramble to the left end of a steep wall. Move up to a

ledge then step left to a block belay.   7) 40ft. The rib and
groove lead pleasantly to the top.

SCRUBBY CRAG   (367115)

This fine steep crag stands at the head of Link Cove (see
Hutaple Crag) and has a sunny south-easterly aspect.
Unfortunately it lies in the main drainage line of the
fellside above and takes several days to dry after rain.
Despite this, and the long approach, the crag is well worth
visiting as it has some of the best routes in the Eastern Fells.
Approach: One of the most daunting approach marches of
any crag in this guide, either by way of Deepdale or by
the north ridge of Hart Crag. Allow at least two hours.
The crag can also be reached from Ambleside via Low
Pike, High Pike, and the summits of Dove Crag and Hart
Crag. (2½ hours, leave sacks on the col between Hart Crag
and Fairfield: the crag is just north of the col).
Topography: The cliff is a steep grooved wall of excellent
rock standing above a plinth of vegetated rocks. A terrace
crosses the cliff above this lower wall and provides access
to the first two routes. In the centre of the crag are two
fine V-grooves, Grendel on the left and Hrothgar on the
right. At the left end of the crag is a steep corner (Juniper
Crack, 165ft., S). Just right of this corner is a curving crack
splitting overhangs, which gives the line of Beowulf.
Descent: Down the slanting rake to the left, or traverse
left to the col.

121   **Beowulf**   **   VS
200ft.   *N. J. Soper and P. E. Brown   1959*
Starts about 30ft. right of Juniper Crack directly below
the curving crack mentioned above.
1) 20ft. A short wall is climbed to a grass ledge.   2) 70ft.
The steep wall above is climbed on small incut holds, first
trending right over a slight bulge then back left into a
shallow groove. Follow this to small stances below the crack.
3) 110ft. Ascend to the overhang, pull into the crack and
climb it to a spike. Traverse right on dubious flakes to the
top of the crag. A fine exposed pitch.

122   **Grendel**   ***   MVS
220ft.   *H. Drasdo and G. Batty   1956*

A superb route taking the left-hand of the two V-grooves in the centre of the crag. Start at the right-hand end of the terrace.

1) 30ft. Climb up to the right to the foot of the groove.
2) 100ft. Mount a flake on the right and traverse left across the groove, and climb it to the long ledge which crosses the upper part of the crag. A superb pitch. 3) 90ft. A short chimney leads to a higher ledge. A recess above is climbed by its right-hand corner, passing a pedestal and moving rightwards to the top of the crag.

123 **Hrothgar** ** HVS
295ft. *N. J. Soper, D. M. Dixon and C. D. Curtis 1960*
A harder sister route to Grendel taking the right-hand V-groove. The start is directly below the groove in a damp vegetated recess reached by 150ft. of scrambling up the right-hand end of the lower tier.

1) 55ft. Step left and up a grassy rake to a short chimney. Climb this and move right to a good grass ledge and nut belays. 2) 140ft. Move diagonally right then back left up a delicate slab to gain the groove, and climb this to a big spike. Mantelshelf onto a wedged block on the left wall and continue up the groove to a good thread in a pocket. The left wall is then climbed to the long ledge. 3) 100ft. Move up to a bilberry ledge, move to its right-hand end and make an exposed move over a bulge (crux) to easy ground.

DOVE CRAG

This large and steep cliff is one of the most forbidding crags in the Lake District. It is finely situated at the head of Dovedale, in relatively remote surroundings. Some of the best extremes in the area are found here and, rather surprisingly, a classic VS and a very good HVD. The rock needs some care and is lichenous—without exception the routes become much harder in wet conditions and take some time to dry out after rain.

Approach: From the car-park and bridge at the north end of Brothers Water, follow the unmade road south past Hartsop Hall. Then take the right-hand footpath up the hillside into Dovedale. The path continues up the valley until a short traverse left leads to the scree at the foot of the

crag. About 1¼ hours.

Descent: Cross the top of the crag and descend at the north end of the right-hand buttress.

124 **Hangover** *** VS

235ft. *J. W. Haggas, J. K. Booth and R. Clough* *1939*

A tremendous climb—exposed and rather serious but a classic of its standard. Start just left of a big boulder at the right-hand side of the slabs between the main buttresses.
1) 6oft. A grassy groove leads to a tree belay in 4oft.; then traverse right to another ledge. 2) 95ft. Climb the corner above. At 4oft. move left for 1oft. using a dubious block, then go up and right over a bulge to regain the corner. Climb the slab and short chimney above; move round the rib on the right to a stance and block belays. (Care—some are loose). 3) 3oft. Traverse right along the exposed ledge, then move up the leaning flake to a stance and small belays. 4) 5oft. Ascend to a groove then move right and climb the V-chimney to the top. This pitch is often rather greasy and strenuous.

125 **Extol** *** XS

350ft. *D. D. Whillans and C. Mortlock* *1960*

A magnificent climb which takes a direct line up the centre of the crag. Both impressive and serious, it is one of the best climbs in the Lake District. Start directly below a chimney in the centre of the crag.
1) 5oft. Broken rock leads to the foot of the chimney.
2) 15oft. Climb the rather vegetated chimney direct. At the top traverse right and go up the little chimney to the good block ledge on Hangover. 3) 15oft. Move down and left then pull onto the main wall. Climb left and up to the foot of a smooth groove. Climb this (hard if greasy) to a small ledge – a good resting place before the next section! Step right and climb the overhanging wall to a big overhang. Move right and pull into a smooth groove with the aid of a peg (in place—out of sight from below). Continue up the groove, then the arete and mossy wall on the right to the top of the crag.

126 **Hiraeth** ** XS

300ft.   *B. Ingle and P. Crew*   1960

An open route of great difficulty wending its way up the
steep wall between Dovedale Groove and Extol. The route
is very exacting but less strenuous than its neighbours.
Start just right of Dovedale Groove at a shallow crack in
a steep slab.

1) 120ft. Climb the crack to a big spike, move right and
step up into a niche. Traverse right on sloping holds
round a large block, into a steep groove. Move up this and
step left onto a grass ledge. The very steep wall and
shallow groove lead to a small stance and piton belays.

2) 50ft. Enter the groove above with difficulty and continue
up this with even more difficulty, passing a small overhang.
The situation now eases and the slab is climbed to a huge
block belay.   3) 50ft. Step left off the block and climb a
steep scoop on small holds to a spike on a slab. Move right
and descend to an exposed stance overlooking the big
corner of Extol. (The downward view is most impressive.)

4) 80ft. Climb back up the groove then up a steeper
groove to the right to a grass ledge. Move right, and
ascend delicately leftwards up the overlapping slab to the top.

127 **Dovedale Groove** * XS

225ft.   *D. D. Whillans, J. Brown and D. Cowan*   1953
Pitches 3 and 4   J. A. Austin and N. J. Soper   1963

A superb and strenuous route—an overhanging groove
followed by an overhanging crack! Start below the obvious
(and exceedingly impressive) line on the left-hand buttress.

1) 75ft. Start the groove with the aid of a sling and nut.
Continue with strenuous bridging and jamming to a stance
and belay below the overhanging crack.   2) 60ft. Climb
the crack to a chockstone, then gain the slab up on the left
by a difficult move. Follow the slab more easily, then take
a groove on the right to a grass rake. Move up this to a
stance and piton belay. It is possible to leave the climb at
this point along the rake.   3) 30ft. Follow the rake up to
the left for a few feet, move back right to a small stance
below an undercut groove. Piton belay.   4) 60ft. A hard
move is made across the overhang to the left (the

51 *Hutaple Crag, West Hutaple Gully is visible to the right;
Curving Gully in the centre of the crag is rather less obvious*

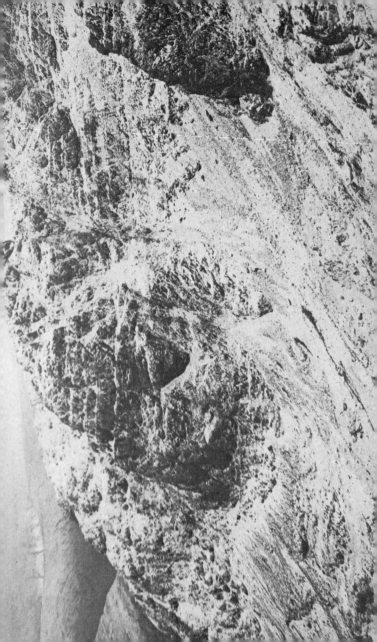

'Western roll' technique is useful here!). Continue with difficulty up the groove to the top of the crag.

128 **Westmorland's Route**   *   HVD
320ft.   *H. Westmorland, J. Mounsey and W. A. North   1910*
This route ascends the ridge at the left-hand end of the main face. A very good climb with some exposed situations. Start at a large boulder at the foot of the ridge.
1) 20ft. Up either side of the boulder to some blocks.
2) 70ft. Move right then climb slabs which eventually lead back to the ridge. Beware of harder, direct variations.
3) 40ft. The ridge leads to a sloping stance.   4) 50ft.
A short crack, then broken rocks to the foot of the wall.
5) 50ft. Climb round to the right to gain a large slab. Follow this diagonally left to a good ledge.   6) 70ft.
Move up a little wall, then follow a gangway left. At the end, climb a steep wall to a large ledge.   7) 40ft. Traverse right along the ledge, then climb a short groove, move left, and finish up the wall above.

WINTER CLIMBING

The eastern side of the Helvellyn-Fairfield chain frequently gives good winter climbing. Because of the altitude and aspect of the high corries, conditions are more reliable here than in the rest of the Lake District. On Helvellyn, Striding Edge is a good winter scramble, for which crampons are occasionally necessary. The gully just on the left of the final slopes also gives a good finish (Grade I). The slopes above Red Tarn give straightforward snow climbing with some steeper alternatives.
Further south in Grisedale the crags at the head of Nethermost Cove and Dollywaggon Cove give several good gully and face climbs (Grade I–III). The gullies of St. Sunday Crag also give some good routes. The high coves of Deepdale and Dovedale offer a variety of gullies, with potentially harder climbs on Hutaple Crag if conditions are very good. There are two gullies here—West Hutaple Gully which is likely to be Grade II, and Curving Gully in the centre of the crag which is around Grade III.

THIRLMERE

This pleasant valley is a good centre, particularly for hardmen! The two crags described below can both be reached in 15 minutes, and have a large choice of hard climbs.

Access

From Penrith and the motorway, turning off down St. John's-in-the-Vale. From Ambleside in the south or Keswick in the north, via the A591. There is a regular bus service through Thirlmere between Keswick and Ambleside.

Accommodation and Camping

Camping and caravanning at Dale Bottom (296218) and Bracken Riggs (299205). The nearest hotels are in Thirlspot and Threlkeld, further hotels at Keswick and Grasmere. There is a YH at Stanah Cross (318190), close to the crags. Further south is a climbing hut (Achille Ratti) on Dunmail Raise (330110).

Food and Drink

Only at the hotels mentioned above and at some local farms. The nearest bar is at Thirlspot (318178), normal licensing hours 11–3, 5.30–10.30 (F., Sat. 11.00), S. 12–2, 7–10.30. There is a PO at Dale Head (317184), but the nearest shops are in Threlkeld and Keswick (EC Wed.). Milk and eggs can be obtained locally.

Garages and Car Hire

The nearest garage for repairs is in Keswick (tel. 72064, closes 6 pm). Some petrol stations in Keswick stay open until 8 pm. Taxis, tel. Keswick 72138, Car hire tel. 72606.

General Services

Telephones at Dale Bottom (296218), and Legburthwaite (318191). The nearest public toilets are in Keswick. There are several climbing shops in both Keswick and Ambleside.

Mountain Rescue

For assistance, ring the local POLICE, giving as much information as possible. They will contact the Mountain Rescue Team which is based at Keswick.

CASTLE ROCK OF TRIERMAIN (322197)

Castle Rock consists of two crags of excellent, steep rock facing west across the southern entrance to St. John's-in-the-Vale. The crags are well seen from the main Ambleside

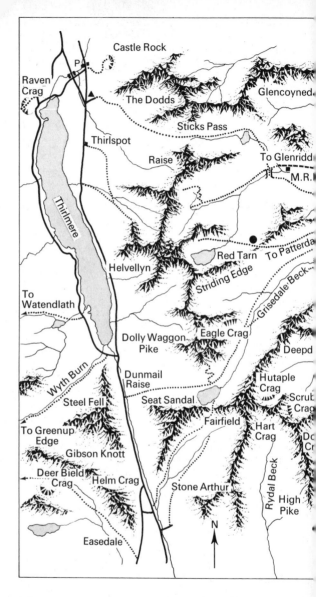

to Keswick road. All the climbs described are in the very
severe category and most are located on the north crag.
This crag, more than anywhere else in the Lakes, offers
very steep climbing on clean rock with incut holds. Strong
fingers are a distinct advantage. The crag dries quickly after
rain and the overhanging nature of the routes gives some
protection against the elements!

Access

From the farm directly below the crag, take the gate
on the right and follow a path through the fields to a
bridge over a conduit (at the left-hand, north end).
Continue through woods to the crag, which is reached in
10 minutes from the road.

Descent: It is probably quickest to the south—round the
end of the south crag. Alternatively circle back and well
round the end of the northerly crags.

129 **North Crag Eliminate** *** XS
260ft. *H. Drasdo and D. Gray 1952*
A superb climb, combining technical difficulty with
considerable exposure. The route follows the overhanging
arete at the left-hand (north) end of the crag and is probably
the finest climb in the Thirlmere area. Start just left of the
wall at the foot of a huge, open groove.
1) 110ft. Gain the groove and follow it for 20ft. before
climbing out leftwards. Move right at the top to reach a
terrace and tree belays.   2) 30ft. Move left and climb a
hidden chimney to a stance behind a large yew tree.
3) 30ft. Climb the tree to the topmost branches! It should
then be possible to reach good handholds and to swing up
and right. Traverse right to a superbly exposed stance and
tree belay.   4) 90ft. Move left to the start of an impressive
gangway. Runner. Climb the gangway with increasing
difficulty to a very welcome large flake. Traverse left round
the corner to a niche. Move delicately up and right onto the
arete which leads to the summit.

52 *Overleaf left: Castle Rock of Triermain*
53 *Overleaf right: The final pitch of North Crag Eliminate, Castle
Rock*

130 **Agony**   ** HVS
27ft.   *G. Oliver and N. Brown*   1959
A splendid, classic climb comprising two long pitches—
first a steep wall, then an overhanging arete. Start at a
break just right of the wall at the north end of the crag.
1) 120ft. Move right and climb the wall on small holds to
the break in the gangway which crosses the wall from right
to left. Traverse horizontally right for about 30ft., then go
directly up a steep groove (peg runner). Continue up the
wall above to an easy traverse line—move right to a tree
belay.   2) 150ft. Move up into the corner above (Overhanging Bastion) then traverse up and right with increasing
difficulty to reach a good ledge (runner). Move awkwardly
left back onto the arete and follow this steeply to gain a
groove above. The groove leads more easily to a huge
slab: traverse this leftwards to the top.

131 **Overhanging Bastion**   *** VS
27ft.   *R. J. Birkett, C. R. Wilson and L. Muscroft*   1939
A tremendous and very exciting climb which follows the
obvious gangway slanting left across the main face (well
seen from the road). It is one of the best climbs at this
standard in the Lake District. Pitch 4 has been poorly
protected since 1939 and should not have peg runners
placed there now! Start 70ft. right of the wall below a holly
1) 40ft. Climb to the holly and pull round it to a ledge.
Move left to some ash trees below a steep corner.   2) 60ft.
Climb the wall for 15ft. then follow the interesting corner to
a good ledge and belay.   3) 40ft. Follow the slab just left
of the continuing corner, until an airy move round to the
left reveals a ledge and pinnacle belay.   4) 65ft. From the
top of the pinnacle make some delicate moves to get onto
the gangway. Follow this more easily (runners) until it ends
Move round left and slightly down onto a very exposed wall
which fortunately has some very good holds. Move left,
then go straight up to a recess and tree belay.   5) 65ft.
Move out of the recess on the right and follow a slab and
easy wall to the top.

54 The end of the Gangway on Overhanging Bastion, Castle Rock

May Day Cracks   *   VS

205ft.   *R. J. Birkett and L. Muscroft*   *1947*

A strenuous and sustained route up the cracks which bisect the north crag.

1) 50ft. As for Overhanging Bastion.   2) 125ft. From the right-hand end of the ledge, ascend the strenuous chimney (often wet) to the remains of a tree. The V-groove above is still difficult, but less strenuous, and leads to a steep wide crack. Climb this and gain a slab on the left. The continuation crack is climbed to a stance and belay.

3) 30ft. The easier crack above to a large ledge. Scramble off to the right or finish up the big slab on the left.

Thirlmere Eliminate   **   XS

185ft.   *P. Ross and P. J. Greenwood*   *1955*

A continuously steep and difficult climb which starts below a large flake some 20ft. right of Overhanging Bastion.

1) 50ft. Climb the right-hand side of the flake, then from the top mantelshelf onto a small ledge. Move right and up a corner to a ledge and belay.   2) 75ft. Traverse left and move up a corner until it is possible to swing left onto the arete. This is followed direct to a sloping ledge and peg belay.   3) 60ft. The impressive corner above. Climb the overhang with a peg for aid then bridge up the steep corner-groove to the top.

Harlot Face   *   HVS

170ft.   *R. J. Birkett and L. Muscroft*   *1949*

Another steep and fingery climb on excellent rock. Start some 50ft. right of Thirlmere Eliminate at a break in the wall.

1) 50ft. Move up to a ledge then start up a corner on the left. Move left again onto the wall which leads steeply to a long narrow ledge. Belay at the right-hand end.   2) 45ft. Climb the overhanging corner for 15ft. then move round the arete on the right. A few moves lead to a large block for runner and rest. Climb the bulging corner to a ledge and tree belays.   3) 20ft. From the top left corner of the ledge go through a crevasse to the foot of a chimney.   4) 55ft. Climb the chimney and continue to the top.

55 Wide bridging up the final groove of Thirlmere Eliminate

Direct Route   MVS
135ft.   *A. T. Hargreaves and G. G. McPhee   1930*
A very enjoyable, steep route. Start just right of the lower
stone wall of the south crag.
1) 35ft. A very steep pitch with some hidden, but very
good, holds. Climb straight up for 20ft., then move left
and up to a small stance.   2) 70ft. Climb the wall to the
sentry box. Step left and continue to a ledge and belay.
3) 30ft. Over a bulge to a slab finish.

RAVEN CRAG, THIRLMERE   (304188)

A large and rather daunting crag which dominates the
north end of Thirlmere lake. It possesses some fine and
impressive climbs. The rock needs rather more care than,
say, Castle Rock and the crag is fairly lichenous, making the
routes slippery in wet conditions and slow to dry after rain.
Access
From the little car-park at the west end of the dam, take
the path through the forest about 100yds. to the north
(to Castle Crag Fort). After about 10 minutes traverse
left through the forest to the foot of the crag.
Descent: Round to the north of the crag, down a grassy gully.

Genesis/Anarchist   *   HS
275ft.   *H. Drasdo and P. Greenwood   1952*
A. Beanland, M. Dawson and E. Leach   1952
A good combination with continuous interest. Starts on the
right-hand buttress, some 20ft. right of a larch tree, and
directly below a bulge and groove.
1) 35ft. Climb the bulge and groove to a stance under an
overhang.   2) 45ft. Go up to an overhang, then move
right and climb a groove and crack to a corner.   3) 30ft.
Climb the corner crack, moving out on the right wall, to a
large ledge and flake belay.   4) 40ft. Straight up the fine
wall.   5) 20ft. Walk left to belay on an oak.   6) 50ft.
Move into the groove on the left of the grass and follow it
to the start of the impressive crack.   7) 55ft. The fine crack
(rather slippery when wet) leads to the final terrace.
A good pitch.

56 Raven Crag, Thirlmere
  A = Approach to the Cave

137 **Totalitarian**   ***   XS

270ft.   *C. J. S. Bonington and M. Thompson   1964*

A particularly fine and varied climb following a continuous steep line. Protection is sometimes poor. Start at the lowest point of the crag and scramble past rowan trees to a large block at the foot of a steep wall.

1) 60ft. A difficult pitch with some poor rock. From the block step left and climb a shallow groove until it is possible to pull onto a small ledge. Step left across the overhanging wall and pull into a niche. Move out right and continue to a good ledge and belay below an open groove.
2) 65ft. Climb the groove to the bulge then gain the slab on the right. Continue up the steep wall to the stance and belay at the end of pitch 1 of Communist Convert.   3) 60ft. Pitch 2 of Communist Convert.   4) 25ft. Climb the groove above leading to a good stance and peg belay below the big roof.   5) 60ft. An impressive final pitch. Traverse right to a smooth slab, which leads up to the edge of the roof. Climb the corner on the left with 1 peg for aid; move right at the top to the foot of an impending crack which is followed to the summit.

138 **Communist Convert**   **   VS

210ft.   *A. R. Dolphin, D. Hopkin and party   1953*

So called because it goes from left to right! An enjoyable, delicate climb taking a diagonal line across the face from the Cave at first. The Direct Finish is described. Start at the foot of an open corner on the right-hand side of the cave. This is reached from a point 30ft. right of the steep grass slope on the left side of the crag. Climb a short chimney-crack then scramble up to the right.

1) 50ft. Ascend the slabs and move right to an exposed stance and belay on the rib.   2) 60ft. Go diagonally right to gain an open groove. This diagonal line is followed via an awkward mantelshelf to a small rock ledge and peg belay.   3) 30ft. Cross a steep wall on the left to a rock ledge. Move down and left to belay on a grass ledge.
4) 70ft. Climb up and right to gain a corner on the left of the big overhangs and follow this to the summit.

57 *Communist Convert, pitch 2*

The Medlar   *   XS

200ft.   *M. Boysen and C. J. S. Bonington   1964*

A fierce climb, both in appearance and in practice! It
ascends the large corner above the left-hand side of the
Cave. Start at a short chimney, about 30ft. right of the
steep grass slope bounding the crag on the left.

1) 25ft. The chimney-crack is followed by a scramble
rightwards to below the centre of the Cave.   2) 40ft.
Climb the leftward-slanting gangway, move right and
ascend to the small medlar tree at the left-hand side of the
Cave.   3) 45ft. Now the climbing gets hard! Move left and
climb the wall to a good foothold below the overhang.
Move left past a good thread runner, then up to a minute
stance and peg belay. It is probably better to continue.
4) 50ft. Climb the corner with 2 pegs for aid, then traverse
left to where difficulties ease. Go up to a good ledge.
5) 40ft. Ascend to a recess, then move up and left before
continuing direct to a grass ledge.   6) 40ft. Climb the
corner-crack above to the top.

WINTER CLIMBING

There is no winter climbing of any importance in the
Thirlmere valley, because of its relatively low altitude.
See the Patterdale section for the nearest reliable
winter climbs.

58 The Medlar, Raven Crag, Thirlmere

This valley has a tremendous variety of crags and climbs to offer at all standards. It is an excellent centre, as in dry weather the high crags (Scafell and Great Gable) are reasonably accessible as well as the local crags. In wet weather (which some expect as 'typical' Borrowdale!) the valley probably has more to offer than any other, particularly on the superb rock of Shepherd's Crag. Some of the crags, but by no means all, are rather vegetated and should be avoided in wet conditions. Borrowdale is often at its best in the winter months, when vegetation and tourists are at a minimum.

Access

The valley can be approached by car from Keswick in the north or from Buttermere over Honister Pass to Seatoller at the south end. The last petrol station is in Keswick. There is a regular bus service up the valley from Keswick— about every 70 minutes in the summer months. During the winter, from 1 November, 6 a day from 6.40 am to 7.20 pm, 9 pm on Saturday only. Borrowdale can also be reached on foot from Ambleside over Greenup, from Langdale over Stake Pass or from Wasdale over Sty Head.

Accommodation and Camping

Camping is restricted to the official site at Keswick (go down the road past the bus station) and to farm campsites at Grange (see approach to Goat Crag), Stonethwaite, Seatoller and Seathwaite. There are several caravan sites in and around Keswick.

The valley is well served by hotels and guest-houses. There is a good selection in Keswick and many others are scattered up the valley. Youth hostels are found at Keswick, at Barrow House (268200), at Grange (247171) and at Longthwaite (254142). There is also a hostel at the summit of Honister Pass (224135). There is an FRCC hut at Rosthwaite and a Northumbrian MC hut near the Bowderstone (255164).

Food and Drink

As well as the hotels and guest-houses, there are restaurants in Keswick and one (licensed) in Seatoller. The latter is closed on Mondays and during the winter months (October to April). Cafés abound for the tourists, particularly in Grange, Seatoller and Seathwaite.

Walla Crag

Rigg Beck

Derwent Water

Falcon Cra

Cat Bells

To Newlands Pass

Little Town

Shepherd's Crag

Gowder Crag

Maiden Moor

Grange

Black Crag

Watendlat

Hindscarth

Great End Crag

Goat Crag

Bowderstone Crag

Grey Buttress

Castle Crag

Dale Head Crag

Miners Crag

Blea Tarn Beck

Dale Head

Rosthwaite

Dock Tarn

Buckstone Howe

Seatoller

Honister

Stonethwaite

Grey Knotts

Comb Gill

Gillercombe

M.R.P.

Seathwaite

Raven Crag

Heron Crag

Eagle Crag

Green Gable

Glaramara

Sergeant Crag

Lining Crag

Stockley Bridge

Greenup Edge

Sty Head Tarn

Long Strath

N

There are shops in Keswick, Grange and Rosthwaite.
Early closing is on Wednesday and market day on
Saturday.
Many of the hotels have only private bars; there are public
bars in Keswick and at the Scafell Hotel in Rosthwaite.
Licensing hours are 11–3, 5.30–10.30 on weekdays, and
12–2, 7–10.30 on Sundays, with 11 pm closing on Fridays
and Saturdays.

Garages and Car Hire

During the day petrol can be obtained at a single pump
at Troutdale cottages (257178). Otherwise one must drive
up to 7 miles into Keswick. For garage repairs, telephone
Keswick 72064 (closes 6 pm). Taxis: telephone Keswick
72138 or 72676. Car hire: telephone Keswick 72606
or 72676.

General Services

There is a tourist information office in the Moot Hall,
Keswick. Here one can hire guides for walking and/or
climbing. There are telephones at Seathwaite, Seatoller,
Rosthwaite and Grange. Toilets are at Keswick, Grange
and Seatoller. Equipment shops of all kinds are found in
Keswick.

Mountain Rescue

For assistance, ring first the local POLICE, giving as much
information as possible. They will contact the Mountain
Rescue team which is based at Keswick. Stretchers and
first-aid kits are available at the following points:
Seathwaite Farm (236121) and Styhead Pass (218095).

FALCON CRAGS (273205)

These impressive and deservedly popular crags have a good
selection of *hard* climbs: all in the VS category and above.
The crags are west-facing and dry quickly (though not as
quickly as Shepherd's Crag). One route is described on the
upper crag, and all the others are found on the lower
buttress. The rock on the climbs described is generally
good, but a watch should be kept for the occasional
loose hold.

Approach: Park in a lay-by two miles from Keswick; the
crags are clearly visible and reached by easy paths in ten
minutes. If the lay-by is full, there is a car park a few
yards up the Watendlath road on the left.

Descent: Obvious and easy grassy slopes to the north of the crags.

140 **Falcon Crag Buttress** ** XS
210ft.   *P. Ross and P. Lockey   1958*
One of the best climbs in Borrowdale in spite of some doubtful rock. Follows a line up the centre of the upper crag via the obvious giant corner. Starts in the centre of the crag above a grassy hump where an oak tree grows.
1) 80ft. Follow the rather loose corner up and right. Continue up a short black groove to a small ledge and peg belay on the right.   2) 70ft. Climb a steep wall for 20ft. to a peg runner, then traverse left and climb a strenuous overhanging crack (peg runner). Continue up the steep wall to a small stance and peg belay below the impressive final corner.   3) 60ft. The first 20ft. of the corner are climbed free, then three pegs are used to reach the final groove. This is entered free with difficulty, then leads more easily to the top.

141 **Spinup** ** VS
145ft.   *P. Ross and D. Sewell   1957*
An exciting climb which starts behind a large ash tree below the left-hand corner of the lower crag.
1) 65ft. Climb the slab leftwards, then go straight up until a gangway leads to a small stance and piton belay.   2) 80ft. Cross the wall on the right with difficulty and climb a steep black groove for 10ft., then step right and descend to gain an exposed traverse above the overhangs. When the traverse ends, climb straight up to the top of the crag.

142 **Hedera Grooves** * MVS
135ft.   *P. Lockey and P. Ross   1956*
A pleasant and quite exposed climb. Start just to the left of the ivy mass.
1) 80ft. Move up to a grass ledge and hawthorn bush, then climb a short steep groove. Traverse right to another groove; climb this then traverse left to a large, obvious holly tree.   2) 55ft. Climb the groove above to a tree stump. (The inhabitant of the huge nest has long since

59 Falcon Crag, Borrowdale

disappeared.) Continue up the gangway on the left to the top of the crag.

143 **Funeral Way** VS
165ft. *P. Ross and P. G. Greenwood 1956*
The route starts about 10oft. right of the ivy mass in a corner just right of an undercut gangway. Tree belay.
1) 75ft. Climb onto the gangway with difficulty using holds on the right wall. Continue up and diagonally leftwards to a flake crack. Climb this to a stance and belays below a groove cutting through the overhangs. 2) 90ft. Easily at first then awkward bridging. At the top of the groove go up left along the exposed gangway to the top of the crag, then traverse back right to belay on a large tree.

144 **The Niche** ** XS
175ft. *A. Liddell and R. McHaffie 1962*
A very fine extreme with technical climbing on excellent rock. Starts 25ft. right of Funeral Way.
1) 65ft. Climb the bulge and the steep wall above for 30ft., then climb a rib on the left to a peg. The intervening 10ft. into the Niche itself (on the right) has been climbed free but usually requires some tension from the rope. Peg belay.
2) 40ft. Climb up the back of the niche before traversing strenuously right to a gap through the overhang. Pull over this, then climb a gangway to a small stance and peg belay.
3) 70ft. Continue up the gangway and wall above.

145 **Dedication** ** XS
160ft. *P. Ross and E. Metcalfe 1957*
A surprisingly delicate climb threading its way through the overhangs which guard the most formidable part of the crag. Start at the same point as the Niche.
1) 60ft. Pull over the bulge then move right to a small ledge. Mantelshelf, then traverse right to a ledge of shattered blocks. 2) 100ft. From the right-hand end of the ledge pull over a small overhang into an open groove. Climb this then step right and move up a few feet, before stepping left onto a fine gangway-corner. Up this until it is possible to move left. Finish up the continuation of the gangway.

60 *The Niche, Falcon Crag*

146 **Illusion** ** HVS
  145ft. *P. Lockey and P. Ross 1956*
  A tremendous, classic climb with a long traverse below the
  huge roof. It starts near the right-hand end of the crag
  on a block behind a high tree.
  1) 25ft. Straight up to a stance and belays. 2) 100ft.
  Climb a steep, awkward groove until it is possible to gain
  a huge flake up on the right. Traverse right to the first of
  several deep grooves. (Runners in the back of these will
  obviously cause rope-drag.) Continue rightwards towards
  the final corner under the roof. When this is reached swing
  round the arete to a ledge and belay. 3) 20ft. An easy
  wall above.

GOWDER CRAG (266187)
An impressive buttress clearly visible from the road near the
Lodore Hotel. It is approached via the tourist path from
the hotel to the waterfall or by a path a few hundred
yards to the north which skirts the hotel grounds (and
avoids payment of the toll!). The rock is good but, once
again, a watch should be kept for loose blocks. The route
described faces the afternoon sun and dries quickly.

147 **Fool's Paradise** ** MVS
  315ft. *P. W. Vaughan and J. D. J. Wildridge 1951*
  A long varied climb with good situations. Start by
  scrambling up for 25ft. to a tree just right of the ridge
  running down to the lowest point of the crag.
  1) 40ft. Follow the corner over blocks to belay on a tree
  under an overhang. 2) 40ft. Traverse delicately left onto
  the ridge and climb this to a large ledge and belay.
  3) 65ft. Descend a little on the right to gain a traverse
  across the slabs. Follow this for some 25ft. then climb up to
  a crack. Make a difficult move right, then find a belay by a
  block on the right, or continue up the next pitch. 4) 50ft.
  Move left into the obvious groove and climb this, taking the
  left-hand branch to a terrace and tree belays. 5) 50ft.
  Traverse right along the terrace to the foot of a deep
  chimney. 6) 70ft. Climb the chimney and pull over the
  overhang. Go up the wall to the final chimney, which is

61 *Fool's Paradise—the difficult move on pitch 3*

awkward to start. A good pitch.

SHEPHERD'S CRAG (264185)

A unique climbing ground! The buttresses provide good pitches for both beginner and tiger and dry very quickly after rain. The rock is generally excellent.

Access to the crags is particularly easy as they are next to the road at a point 4 miles from Keswick just past the Lodore Hotel.

There are a great many climbs here apart from the ones described; most of these would be obvious on further exploration. The climbs are described from left to right and are reached by a short walk through the wood from the top of the little hill 100yds. south of the Lodore Hotel.

148 **Brown Crag Wall** * S

190ft.   *R. Wilkinson and K. C. Ogilvie   1950*

A good climb on the wall at the north end of Shepherd's Crag. It starts on polished holds about 75ft. right of the fence and about 20ft. left of a very steep groove (Conclusion, XS).

1) 50ft. Climb up into a slippery little corner then move out right and up steeply to a ledge and peg belay.   2) 70ft. Traverse left for 10ft. then go up the fine wall, slightly left, until it is possible to traverse 20ft. right to a tree belay.

3) 70ft. Climb the steep but pleasant scoop running diagonally left to the top of the crag.

149 **Brown Slabs Arete** * D

150ft.   *C. D. Frankland and Bentley Beetham   1922*

On the slabs just round the corner from Brown Crag Wall are three popular climbs. This one starts near the left-hand end of the slabs and goes up and diagonally left for 50ft. to a conspicuous notch, then climbs the ridge in two pitches.

150 **Brown Slabs Direct** VD

130ft.   *Bentley Beetham   1948*

This climb starts about 20ft. right of the Arete climb and goes directly up the slabs in three pitches.

151 **Brown Slabs** D

130ft. *Bentley Beetham* *1946*

Starts about 30ft. left of the very polished corner-crack. It goes up a fault past two trees, then takes the easiest line up the upper slab to belay on the top.

152 **Ardus** ** S

120ft. *V. Veevers, H. Westmorland and P. Holt* *1946*

Walk south from Brown Slabs along the path until a large buttress is reached. Ardus climbs the wide couloir/gully on the left of the main wall, finishing up an exciting slab. Start by moving up from the path to a ramp going diagonally right.

1) 55ft. Climb across the ramp rightwards then go up to belay in the gully below a huge block. 2) 30ft. Climb over the block and continue direct to a large ledge and belays. 3) 35ft. Traverse left across the exposed slab and climb the first crack reached to the top. The second crack, 10ft. further left, is slightly easier. Tree belay.

153 **Eve** * VS

155ft. *W. Peascod and R. Blake* *1951*

Starts about 50ft. right of Ardus behind a tree and beside a split block.

1) 40ft. Climb a slab and steep crack to a ledge and block belays. 2) 65ft. Up into the corner, then make a long stride left onto the rib. Go diagonally left across the big slab, with an awkward mantelshelf *en route*, to a small stance and nut belays. 3) 50ft. Climb up the rib steeply, then go right following the obvious crack with good hand-holds and lots of exposure to the top of the crag.

154 **Adam** * HVS

135ft. *P. Ross and R. Wilkinson* *1955*

A steep pitch, one of the best hereabouts, with good holds. Start in a corner some 20ft. right of Eve.

1) 35ft. Climb the crack on good jams to the large ledge and block belays. 2) 100ft. Move up a polished wall on the right to a large runner. Then go left and up to gain a steep crack. Climb this then move right steeply to reach the holly tree. Climb up behind the tree (or the groove on the right) into a corner. Pull out left and climb the steep wall above to finish at the same point as Eve.

155 Kransic Crack Direct   HVS

100ft. · *G. B. Fisher, D. Oliver and F. Bantock (without direct finish) 1952*

The path south from the start of Adam arrives after several hundred yards at a steep, obvious crack forming the left-hand side of a huge flake.

1) 100ft. Climb the excellent jamming crack to the top of the large flake. Traverse right along the flake then across a steep wall. Then move up and back left onto the wall above the flake and climb this directly to the top.

(The groove on the left of Kransic Crack is *Fisher's Folly*— VS. Climb the groove to a ledge and belay. Then make a long traverse right to finish at the same point as Kransic Crack Direct.)

156 Little Chamonix   *   VD

205ft. *Bentley Beetham 1946*

A deservedly popular climb. About 7ft. right of Kransic Crack there is a chimney from which grows an oak. Start about 20ft. right of this chimney.

1) 25ft. Climb a short crack to a ledge. 2) 65ft. Move onto a corner on the left, then go up to gain a ramp leading up diagonally left to a large grassy terrace. 3) 40ft. Scramble rightwards to a corner below impressive grooves. 4) 40ft. Up the left-hand groove and climb over the block in a sitting position! Traverse the slab on the right and go up the arete to belays. 5) 35ft. Climb the steep wall to a pinnacle then make an exposed move right to reach a chimney which leads easily to the top. Tree belays.

BLACK CRAG (263174)

This superb large crag dominates the tiny valley of Troutdale and provides excellent climbing at all standards on good rock. It is divided into two buttresses by a vegetated gully. The right-hand buttress provides wall, groove and slab climbing and all the routes in the lower grades. Troutdale Pinnacle has tremendous variety and is one of the best climbs in Borrowdale. The left-hand buttress is steeper, with a band of overhangs, and several hard climbs.

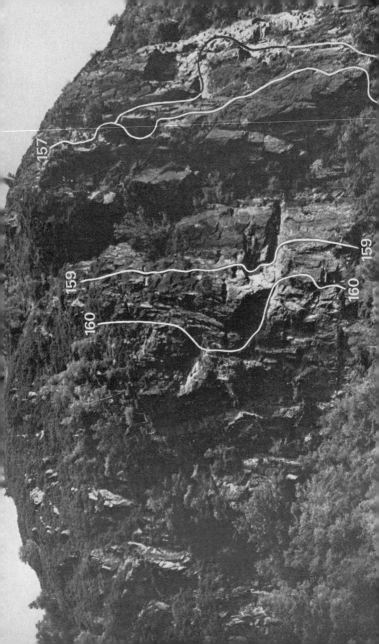

Approaches: There are two. The easiest is from Derwent View (mid-way between the Borrowdale Hotel and Grange). A narrow lane leads left from the double bend into Troutdale, from where a path leads directly up to the crag. About 20 minutes. Cars should be left on the main road 100yds. south of the lane entrance. Alternatively, from the Bowderstone car-park (253168) follow paths north-east over a little col into Troutdale. About 30 minutes to the crag.

Descent: From the top of the climbs traverse the top of the crag to the south to join a good path descending from the col diagonally back to the foot of the crag.

157 **Troutdale Pinnacle**   ***   HVD
360ft.   *F. Mallinson and R. Mayson   1914*
This well-established classic climb starts where the footpath meets the foot of the crag either at a broken chimney or up a crack on the right. It is rather harder, but still enjoyable, on a wet day.

1) 25ft. The chimney or crack leads to a ledge with a belay at the right-hand end.   2) 45ft. Climb a wall and a shallow groove to a large block belay.   3) 95ft. Follow polished holds up a groove on the right onto the slabs. Climb these rightwards to belay below a short corner.
4) 35ft. Move up the corner then left onto a higher slab. Small stance and thread belay.   5) 70ft. Traverse left, across and down the slab to the wall impasse (small stance and belay possible on the slab a few feet down). Climb the short, steep section on polished but good holds. Easier ledges soon lead to good belays.   6) 30ft. The wall above to the top of the Pinnacle.   7) 60ft. Ascend the corner up the steep ridge with good protection finishing with an exciting move left to high footholds. Easily thereafter to a ledge and belays.

158 **Troutdale Pinnacle Superdirect**   HVS
365ft.   *P. Ross and D. Oliver   1954*
A fine varied climb which starts at the centre of a slab 20ft. left of the previous climb.

1) 40ft. Climb the slab to a large ledge and belays.
2) 75ft. The steep crack above leads to a narrow ledge.

63 Black Crag, Borrowdale

Traverse right to a large block belay.   3) 80ft. Climb the
wall above, moving left occasionally, to a small ledge and
belays below a superb-looking crack.   4) 75ft. The fine,
steep crack.   5) 35ft. Move up into a polished groove then
gain with difficulty an obvious finger-traverse on the right.
Those with thin fingers have a distinct advantage on this
traverse, which is followed to an easier groove which leads
to the top of the pinnacle.   6) 60ft. As for last pitch of
previous route.

159 **Vertigo**   *   HVS
    260ft.   *P. Ross and W. Aughton*   *1958*
    A highly enjoyable climb taking the obvious break in the
    overhangs on the left-hand buttress. Start below the centre of
    the buttress.
    1) 40ft. A grassy scramble and some wet ledges lead to a
    belay on a yew tree below the steep wall.   2) 50ft. The
    steep break on the left is climbed directly to the traverse
    line across the wall. Move left to a peg belay below the
    huge roof.   3) 40ft. Move back right to below the break
    in the overhangs. Gain the crack by means of a mantel-
    shelf and follow it moving out right at the top, over the
    overhang, onto an exposed ledge. This pitch has been climbed
    free but most people use one peg for aid. Peg belay.   4) 130ft
    Climb the steep wall (1 peg) and move left onto the rib.
    Follow this more or less directly to the summit. This could
    be a hard pitch in greasy conditions.

160 **The Shroud**   VS
    240ft.   *P. Ross and P. Lockey*   *1958*
    A varied climb which is however rather mossy and slow to
    dry. Starts at the foot of a steep groove at the northern end
    of the left-hand buttress.
    1) 40ft. Climb the fine groove to a ledge and belay on the
    right.   2) 50ft. Follow a shallow groove on the left to an
    overhang. Move right and up to the peg belay under the
    large overhang.   3) 70ft. Traverse left for about 25ft. then
    go straight up over a small overhang. Continue steeply;
    pass another small overhang on the left and climb a short
    groove to a grass ledge and peg belay.   4) 80ft. Gain a rib
    on the right and follow slabs and grooves rightwards to a
    bulge. Move right and continue more easily to the top.

GREAT END CRAG   (260170)

This crag, which is heavily vegetated, has been the scene of several large fires. The centre of the crag has recently been scoured of vegetation, cleaned and brushed to yield several new climbs. The rock hereabouts needs care.

Approach: From Troutdale using either of the approaches to Black Crag. Go directly up the hillside to the foot of the crag. Time 30 minutes.

Descent: A good path leads down through the trees on the east (Black Crag) side.

161 **Great End Pillar**   **   HVS

300ft.   *C. Read, J. Adams, R. McHaffie and B. Henderson   1969*
A route with continuous interest which starts in the centre of a pillar on the left.

1) 50ft. Climb the wall and step left into a small groove. Up this and continue to a ledge.   2) 80ft. Climb the steep wall above (peg for aid), eventually moving left to a spike. Then continue up the arete to a large stance.   3) 60ft. Above are three grooves. Climb the obvious right-hand groove to a stance and belay.   4) 110ft. A good pitch. Straight up the layback flake to a ledge. Surmount an embedded flake and climb a short corner. Pull out left and move up steep rock onto an arete which leads to the top. Belay well back.

161A **Great End Corner**   ***   HVS

250ft.   *D. S. Nichol, C. Downer, I. Conway and A. Hellier 1975*
A good route, well protected. Starts below the corner in the centre of the crag.

1) 50ft. Climb the corner to a ledge on the left. Tree root belay.   2) 150ft. Climb the bed of the corner to a short smooth groove. Piton runner. Climb the groove (delicate) or the crack on the left wall to a line of large flakes. Continue up the corner to a ledge. Piton belay.   3) 50ft. Move left into the undercut groove and after a difficult pull continue more easily to the top.

64   Overleaf left: Great End Crag, Borrowdale

65   Overleaf right: Eagle Crag, Borrowdale

EAGLE CRAG (277122)

This is the steep crag facing north across Greenup Ghyll, with an impressive profile well seen from Stonethwaite and the main Borrowdale road. The steepness and exposure, together with the excellent nature of the rock, make for some of the finest and hardest routes in the valley. All the routes here are in the VS category or above.

Approach: From Stonethwaite cross the bridge and follow the Greenup path along the north side of the river. Leave the path near some sheep-folds, then cross the stream and go diagonally rightwards across the fellside to the foot of the crag.

Descent: Round the east end of the crag and down the true left bank of a wide grassy gully. There is another relatively small crag on the east side of the gully.

162 **The Great Stair** MVS

26oft.   *W. Peascod and S. E. Beck 1946*

At the east end of the crag a short rake ascends from left to right. Start about 25ft. up the rake.

1) 50ft. Climb the wall past the tree to a ledge. Go straight up the second wall for a few feet, then diagonally right to a second small ledge and belay.   2) 35ft. Diagonally left up the third wall to a large grass platform.   3) 55ft. A steep wall with small holds leads to a ledge. Follow a diagonal line left to a grass terrace with a thread belay on the left arete.   4) 55ft. A smooth wall is climbed rightwards to turf ledges which lead to the foot of a fine chimney.   5) 65ft. The pleasant chimney leads to the top.

163 **Falconer's Crack**   *   VS

22oft.   *W. Peascod and S. B. Beck 1946*

A classic climb involving a strenuous crack and delicate wall climbing. Start on the left of some steep corners left of the centre of the crag.

1) 25ft. The crack has good holds and leads to a ledge and belay.   2) 35ft. The narrow 'two step' crack is climbed over a bulge.   3) 30ft. The groove above leads to a niche and belay near a peregrine's nest.   4) 6oft. Move 15ft. left to gain a rib, then climb the wall beyond. Easier climbing then leads to a belay below the chimney of Great Stair.   5) 70ft. Climb the face on the right of the chimney, finishing up a slab.

164 **Daedalus** ** XS

160ft.   *P. Nunn, B. L. Griffiths and P. Ross   1965*

A steep, impressive climb with considerable difficulties.
Start below a very steep chimney in the steep corners to
the right of Falconer's Crack. The route follows a thin
crack up the green wall before finishing up the steep
final wall.

1) 100ft. Gain a ledge below the chimney. Climb the
chimney and the ramp above to a tree. Ascend a bulge into
a steep groove. Use a piton to climb the groove then go up
the wall above moving right to good holds. Climb diagonally
rightwards to a triangular ledge and peg belay.   2) 60ft.
Step left and climb the steep wall to a slight groove (sling
for aid). Continue up the groove to the top.

165 **Post Mortem** * XS

140ft.   *P. Ross and P. Lockey   1956*

Although not a long climb, Post Mortem is notorious as one
of the most strenuous climbs in the Lake District. There are
probably more tales of jammed knees, upside-down moves
and involuntary descents associated with this climb than
with any other! Start directly below the overhanging crack.

1) 80ft. Follow a flake rightwards then continue to a large
ledge and tree belay.   2) 60ft. The Crack. After the initial
20ft. it is usual to rest on a sling round the chockstone.
Continue strenuously, by layback at first, up the fine crack
to the top.

166 **Inquest** * HVS

220ft.   *P. Ross and P. Nunn   1965*

Follows an impressive line on the right-hand edge of the
crag. Start on the right of Post Mortem.

1) 50ft. Climb over ledges, traversing up to the right to some
doubtful blocks. Traverse left across a slab and over grass
to a ledge and belay.   2) 110ft. Move right from the ledge
until a line of handholds leads up to a steep corner. Climb
this then traverse right on good holds to an overhang, and
using a peg for aid gain a steep exposed groove. Move into
the corner and go up to a stance and belay.   3) 60ft.
From the right end of the ledge go up easily then move
left. Continue to the top via a wide crack and easier rock.

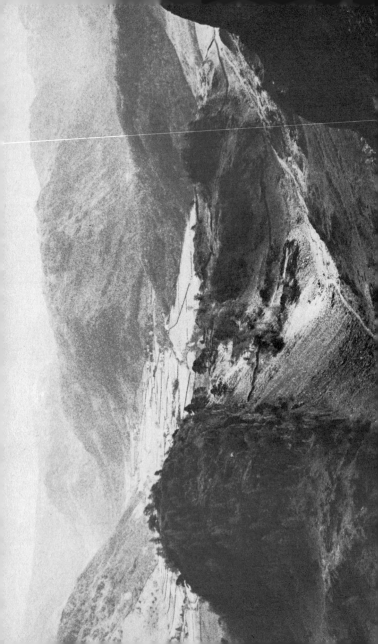

RAVEN CRAG (248114)

A large, rather broken crag in a good situation facing north-east over Combe Ghyll. It offers one of the best climbs of 'Difficult' standard in the Borrowdale valley.

Approach: From Mountain View cottages, where the main road crosses the river, follow the Thornythwaite Farm road. After about 100yds., cross a stile on the left and follow the good path. At the entrance to Combe Ghyll a fainter path goes left and leads diagonally across the fellside to the foot of the crag. Total time—45 minutes.

Descent: Follow a grass ramp behind a stone wall and the subsequent path round the south-east end of the crag.

167 **Raven Crag Gully** ** VD

510ft. *W. Wilson and J. W. Robinson 1893*

The most obvious feature of the crag is a classic gully, usually wet, providing strenuous climbing and (for an enthusiastic party) much enjoyment. Note that in wet weather the severe alternative to pitch 8 would almost certainly have to be taken. The gully is at its very best in a hard winter (up to Grade IV).

1) 75ft. Moderate climbing on the right to a cave under a chockstone which is climbed on the right. 2) 70ft. A groove on the right side of the gully is climbed for 55ft., then traverse across the gully to its left side. 3) 65ft. Up the groove on the right wall, then easy climbing on the left. 4) 45ft. Scrambling. 5) 70ft. A rib on the right of the gully is followed to a cave at 40ft. Pass this on the right to a belay. 6) 100ft. Scrambling, apart from a 15ft. wall. 7) 50ft. Up the right wall to a chockstone then traverse awkwardly right to a belay. 8a) 35ft. Climb up a few feet, then traverse into the gully below the Capstone, which is climbed on the left to the top. 8b) 30ft. Severe. Climb the steep rocks direct from the belay.

168 **Corvus** *** D

450ft. *Bentley Beetham 1950*

A very good, continuously interesting climb. From Raven Crag Gully in the centre of the crag find the second gully to the left (south) and start a few feet left of this.

1) 60ft. Straight up the slabs for 50ft., then move right

66 Castle Crag and Upper Borrowdale from Goat Crag. Eagle Crag and Raven Crag can be seen top left and top right respectively

around the corner to a good belay in the gully.   2) 30ft.
Climb the left wall of the gully to belay on a good ledge.
3) 35ft. Traverse left along the broad ledge to the foot of a
groove.   4) 8oft. Climb the corner on good holds, then go
up the steep chimney. Finally, ascend easily rightwards to a
good stance.   5) 95ft. Move 2oft. right, then climb a rib
on good holds to belay at the foot of a wall.   6) 25ft.
Traverse left across the steep wall on flake handholds to a
big ledge. Belay.   7) 45ft. A short wall then easy rocks to
a terrace.   8) 4oft. The rib above to a belay below a
scoop.   9) 4oft. Continue up the scoop to the top of the
crag.

GILLERCOMBE   (221124)

The combe contains a relatively large crag and the
pleasant buttress route is traditionally used as an approach
to routes on Gable Crag.
Approach: From Seathwaite cross the river and go up the
steep fellside on the left of Sourmilk Ghyll. Continue into
the combe when the crag appears on the far side to the
north-west. Time: approx. 1 hour. A faster approach begins
at Honister summit. Follow an indefinite path diagonally
leftwards to a shallow col on the skyline. The crag is then
straight ahead and is easily reached in 30 minutes.
Descent: Skirt around either end of the crag.

169   **Gillercombe Buttress**   ***   MS
360ft.   *H. B. Lyon and W. A. Woodsend   1912*
A pleasant and popular climb. Start just to the right of an
obvious gully near the centre of the crag.
1) 45ft. Climb up steeply to a square recess on the left.
Continue up the right wall to a stance and belay.   2) 45ft.
Ascend to the left of the belay for 2oft., then traverse up
right across a mossy slab to a belay.   3) 35ft. Traverse left
for 2oft., then climb easy rocks to a belay on the left.
6oft. of scrambling leads to the start of the next pitch.
4) 35ft. Go left to the foot of an open chimney.   5) 6oft.
Climb the chimney, then go up to the right to a stance.
6) 35ft. Ascend a short steep corner to a large ledge.
Another bout of scrambling leads in 8oft. to a large
bilberry corner.   7) 3oft. Step left from a flake of rock and

67   *The hand-traverse on Corvus (Pitch 6) Raven Crag,*
Combe Ghyll

climb a groove to a ledge. Belay on the left. 8) 50ft.
Climb slabs to the foot of a small chimney. Belay on the
right. 9) 25ft. Continue up the slabs on the right of the
chimney to the top of the crag.

GOAT CRAG (NORTH) (245165)

Not many crags were 'discovered' as recently as the
northerly end of Goat Crag. The routes were literally dug
out of vegetation following Les Brown's discovery of
Praying Mantis in 1965.
The crag is very large but still holds quantities of vegetation
Where this has been removed, the routes are generally of
very good quality. The crag faces north and the routes dry
relatively slowly.

Approach: Easily seen from Grange, the crag is best reached
by following an unsurfaced road south-west from the café
at Grange for ½ mile to a campsite (249168). Cross the
campsite (west) to a stile, then follow a narrow path along
the top of the woods until the crag can be approached
directly. Only 15 minutes from the campsite. Most of the
climbs start from a rocky rake slanting up below the crag.
Descent: Descend easy rakes to the south and skirt below
all the crags—rather long if the party is returning for
another climb. On some routes it is quicker to descend by
abseil.

170 **The Peeler** * VS
270ft. *B. Henderson, D. McDonald and J. Cook* *1965*
An enjoyable climb up a prominent crack and groove on
sound rock. Start by scrambling up left from the ramp to a
prominent yew tree belay at the foot of the obvious crack.
1) 100ft. Move left from the yew tree into the crack.
Follow this to a good stance and tree belay. 2) 70ft.
Ascend the cleaned corner groove until a break left can be
made to a holly tree. Belay. The best climbing ends here,
and it is possible to descend by abseil from this point.
3) 40ft. Climb a corner over perched blocks to a large
flake; go up this to belay. 4) 60ft. Easy climbing and
scrambling leads to the top.

171 **D.D.T.** ** HVS
220ft. *J. Lee, A. Jackman and P. Ross* *1965*
Much further up the ramp from the foot of the Peeler is an

68 DDT and Praying Mantis, Goat Crag, Borrowdale

impressive corner to the right of an undercut buttress.
D.D.T. follows this corner. Protection is rather poor on the
first pitch.

1) 120ft. Climb the corner and turn a bulge on the right.
Continue up the groove and fine crack to a ledge and piton
belay. 2) 100ft. Move right up a short wall into the deep
groove. Follow this to a steeper section which leads onto an
upper slab. Go diagonally left to tree belays. Continue by
long heathery scrambling, or abseil off using convenient
trees.

172 **Praying Mantis** *** HVS
260ft. *L. Brown and J. S. Bradshaw 1965*
A really splendid climb with a tremendous variety of
climbing and some of the best situations in Borrowdale.
The route is strenuous at first, but as the exposure increases,
it becomes more delicate. Start in a groove some 50ft.
right of the route followed by D.D.T.

1) 75ft. Move up to a large flake. Climb the crack and
groove with difficulty to a narrow niche. Step left onto a
slabby wall and gain the slab above by a step to the right.
Climb the slab to a tree belay. 2) 50ft. Follow the grass
rake up to the left, then cross a smooth wall into a groove.
Go up this for 15ft. until a step right leads to a good stance
and peg belay on the face of the buttress. 3) 25ft.
Traverse right to a small exposed stance and peg belay.
4) 110ft. Climb the wall diagonally right for a few feet to
a good thread runner. Ascend directly up the steep wall
above, eventually stepping left onto the final slab. Follow
this to a heather terrace and tree belay.

173 **Bitter Oasis** *** HXS
150ft. *P. J. Livesey and party 1975*
This magnificent, and extremely difficult route goes up the wall
to the right of Praying Mantis. The difficulties are of a high
order and are sustained throughout. Start about 25ft. above
and right of Praying Mantis behind a tree.

1) 90ft. Step off the tree and go up to a peg runner. Pull onto a
little slab on the left then move right to an undercut hold. Enter
the groove above and climb this to another peg runner.
Continue awkwardly to a bulge and climb this, using the only
jugs on the route, to gain a slab which leads with surprising

69 Just below the crux on the first pitch of Praying Mantis, Goat Crag

difficulty to a small haven on the right edge of the buttress.   2) 60ft. Move up to a peg runner then traverse left to a downward-pointing spike. Move round this and up the groove above to a bolt runner on the left. A very hard move up the short wall above leads to a few feet of easier climbing and the top.

174   **Monsoon**   VS
210ft.   *G. Oliver and C. Griffiths   1966*
This is the chimney-groove bounding the main buttress on the right.
1) 80ft. Scramble up ledges to the right of Bitter Oasis to a stance below the chimney.   2) 130ft. Climb the chimney to the overhang, step right and continue in the same line until a traverse right leads to a rib. Go up this for a few feet then back left to a narrow slab which completes the climb.

WINTER CLIMBING

GREAT END   (227085)
This is the most accessible high crag and is approached directly up Grains Ghyll from Seathwaite. The traditional gullies give very good winter climbs. Care should be taken to establish that conditions are good, and that there is no avalanche danger in Central Gully. The best descent (particularly in the dark!) is to skirt round all the crags eastwards towards Esk Hause.

Cust's Gully   Grade I.
200ft.
The right-hand (westerly) gully gives a straightforward slope, with possibly one small ice pitch, under an impressive wedged chockstone arch.

Central Gully   Grade I–II.
600ft.   *W. P. Haskett-Smith   1882*
A fine winter climb. Follow the gully to a definite fork. The right branch (normal route) usually has a short, steep ice pitch followed by a slope of hard snow. The left fork can offer a good long ice pitch (sometimes Grade III).

70 *Great End, showing Central and South-East Gullies*

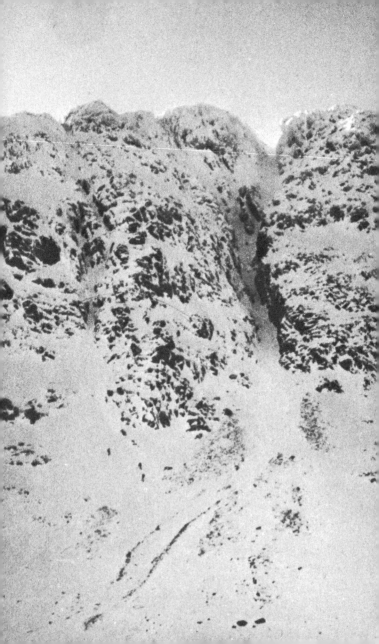

South-east Gully   Grade I–II.

600ft.   *W. P. Haskett-Smith   1882*

Rather less obvious than Central Gully; on the left of the latter. Start easily on snow slopes to an ice pitch at about 200ft. This is usually turned on the right. Traverse back into the gully and continue, usually on steep snow.

Buttresses

In suitable conditions the buttresses of Great End can offer exciting climbs. When the gullies are full of people, try for example the buttress on the right of Central Gully at about Grade I–II.

GABLE CRAG   (213105)

This is easily accessible from the top of Honister Pass along the slopes of Brandreth, and is often in good condition. The crag is described in the Wasdale section.

OTHER CLIMBS

The next highest winter-climbing ground is Gillercombe, where slight gullies at around Grade I are the usual order of the day. In hard winters an entertaining approach via Sourmilk Ghyll could be made. All other crags in Borrowdale are distinctly low for winter-climbing and a hard winter is required. (If in doubt—Derwentwater should be frozen solid!) Then Raven Crag Gully becomes a superb ice-climb (Grade III–IV) with three big pitches. Sergeant Crag Gully also presents a challenging climb. Further exploration is left to the reader in a suitable winter.

71 Below the main pitch, Central Gully, Great End

This area gives a varied selection of climbs of all grades (except the highest) on mountain crags set in beautiful surroundings. Few climbers visit the area, which is relatively remote, and with the exception of Buckstone How it is still unusual to share a crag with another party. In poor conditions the higher crags can be rather greasy and slow to dry, and protection is not always adequate, making the climbs a serious proposition. However, climbers can easily reach the more sheltered crags of Borrowdale over Honister Pass.

Access

To Buttermere, by road from Keswick and Borrowdale via Newlands or Honister Pass, or from the West Coast via Crummock Water. The crags at the head of the Newlands valley are quickly reached from the top of Honister Pass, or by driving and walking up the Newlands valley from Stair. There is a bus service from Cockermouth to Buttermere, daily in the summer but only on Monday and Saturday at other times. An alternative approach is to take the bus from Keswick to Seatoller and walk over Honister Pass (5 miles to Buttermere village). The nearest railway station is at Workington, 18 miles.

Accommodation and Camping

The most convenient campsite for the crags is at Gatesgarth farm (194149) at the foot of Honister Pass, but for those who prefer to camp nearer the pub there are sites in Buttermere village. There are two hotels in Buttermere village and several farms and guest houses in the area offering accommodation. There is also a Youth Hostel in the village and one on the summit of Honister Pass, and an F.R.C.C. climbing hut at Hassness (186158). In the Newlands valley there are several hotels and guest houses at Braithwaite, Stair and Swinside.

Food and Drink

The two hotels in Buttermere village serve meals, drinks and bar snacks, and several of the farmhouses sell teas and snacks. There is also a snack bar in the village. Many climbers drink in the large bar at the Fish Hotel in Buttermere, though the Kirkstile Hotel at Loweswater (142210) is well worth a visit. Licensing hours 11–3, 5.30–10.30 (Fri., Sat. 11.00), S. 12–2, 7–10.30. The nearest

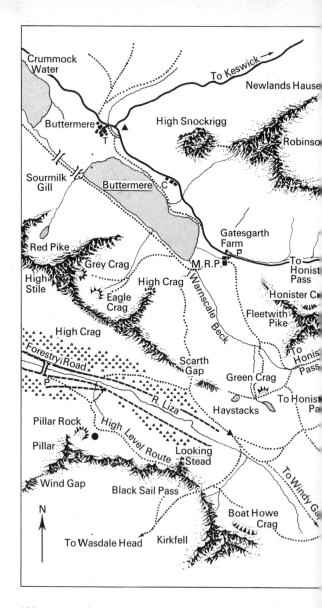

shop is at Lorton (162255) although there is a PO in Buttermere village and both the farm at Gatesgarth and the snack bar at Buttermere sell milk and eggs.

Garages and Car Hire

There are some petrol pumps in Buttermere village, but the nearest breakdown and repair services are in Keswick (see preceding chapter) or at Castle Motors in Cockermouth (tel. 3391) which is open until 6 pm.

General Services

Mostly poor: there is a telephone in Buttermere village but Keswick is the nearest place with climbing shops.

Mountain Rescue

For assistance ring the local POLICE (999) or go to the MR post at Gatesgarth Farm (194149, tel. Buttermere 256).

BUCKSTONE HOW (223143)

This crag, with its sunny aspect and short approach, is one of the most popular crags in the area. The routes vary in length from 150–300ft., but all are hard. The rock is steep and the holds frequently suspect or alarmingly smooth, which makes for an unusually serious feeling on most climbs. In compensation the protection is usually quite good and the rock dries rapidly after rain.

Approach: Park at the top of Honister Pass, and take an old quarry track which leads NW to a quarry spoil heap and old cableway. Cross these and descend slightly to the foot of the crag. 10 mins.

Descent: Traverse right and descend the slanting rake which forms the top edge of the crag. Much loose material lies on this rake and great care must be exercised to avoid dislodging stones onto parties on the cliff below.

175 **Groove Two**   *   VS

150ft.   *W. Peascod and S. B. Beck   1947*

About 70ft. left of the extreme right of the crag is a pair of clean cut grooves, set one above the other and separated by a large terrace. The rock is sound but the climb is harder than it looks!

72 *Overleaf left: Buckstone How from Honister Crag, Buttermere*

73 *Overleaf right: Cleopatra, Buckstone How*

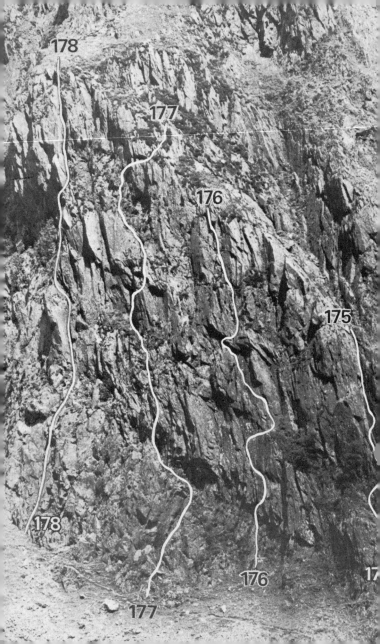

1) 60ft. The first groove leads to the terrace. Belay by a birch tree. 2) 90ft. Climb the right wall of the groove for a few feet until a subsidiary groove on the left can be entered. Climb this until a very awkward move enables the main groove to be regained. Continue up this (still interesting) to the large rake.

176 **Cleopatra** ** HVS

230ft. *W. Peascod and B. Blake 1949*

This fine climb is one of the best of its standard in the area. It combines steep climbing on reasonably sound rock with good protection, fine situations and sustained interest. About 80ft. left of Groove Two a grassy gangway slants up to the left below the large overhangs. Start just right of this up a broken rib.

1) 80ft. Climb the rib to a runner then go diagonally rightwards over the overhang onto a gangway. Follow this up to the left to a crack which is followed for a few feet until an airy traverse on pockets can be made across the wall on the right to a large stance. Piton belay recommended 2) 65ft. Make an awkward move up the rib on the left then traverse left into the left-hand of two grooves. Climb this using a dubious spike and step left to a good belay but poor stance. 3) 85ft. A difficult move over the overhang on the right is followed by easier climbing up the groove above to the top of the crag.

177 **Honister Wall** ** HS

285ft. *W. Peascod and S. B. Beck 1946*

A good climb although care is needed with some of the holds. The route starts up a clean wall just right of a large block on the path at the foot of the crag, some 60ft. left of Cleopatra.

1) 60ft. Climb the wall, stepping right at any difficulties, to the rake below the overhangs. Move left to a stance and various doubtful belays. 2) 85ft. Traverse left across a steep open groove and climb a steep arete to a niche. Step right and continue directly via a short groove to a large recess. 3) 40ft. The Black Wall. Climb the corner to a good runner then traverse strenuously right to the rib and move up to a belay on the right. 4) 60ft. Climb diagonally leftwards under a small overhang and up broken ground to a stance and poor belays. 5) 40ft.

Climb diagonally rightwards to the top of the crag.

178 **Sinister Grooves** ** VS

250ft.   *W. Peascod and S. B. Beck   1948*

A climb of great character up the highest part of the crag.
Start some 35ft. left of the large block directly below a
conspicuous and deeply cut V-groove at 100ft.
1) 80ft. A steep wall and shallow groove lead with
increasing difficulty to a good stance below the groove.
2) 40ft. The smooth groove is climbed with some difficulty
to a stance on the left.   3) 40ft. The loose rib above is
climbed to a large recess and good belay below a line of
cracks and chimneys.   4) 90ft. The easy looking crack
proves smooth and quite strenuous. After 20ft. the chimney
is entered and followed steeply, but on good holds, to the
top of the crag.

EAGLE CRAG   (172145)

Standing in a commanding position at the head of
Birkness Combe is Eagle Crag, the largest cliff in the area.
The rock is perfect, but as the crag faces north it is rather
slow to dry. This means the climbs can be very greasy, and
although Eagle Front can be done in the rain, it is generally
advisable to pick a dry day to visit this excellent crag.
Approach: From Gatesgarth farm a level track across the
fields is followed through a gate. A few yards up the hillside
the Birkness Combe path branches off to the right below a
small broken crag and slants up into the Combe itself. The
path follows the general line of the stream which drains
the Combe until a final scree slope leads to the foot of the
crag ($1\frac{1}{4}$ hours).
Descent: Down the loose scree gully to the west of the crag.

179 **Carnival** ** HVS

500ft.   *N. J. Soper, J. A. Austin and I. Roper   1965*

A poorly protected climb of great character. The climb
takes a line of cracks and grooves immediately right of
Central Chimney (VS) and commences up broken rock
some 80ft. left of the point where the crag bends round
into the deep scree gully which bounds it on the right.
1) 100ft. Easy scrambling left leads to a recess below an
impending crack.   2) 45ft. The crack is climbed with

difficulty, finishing with a short layback, to a block belay
below a shallow groove.   3) 70ft. Step down to the right
and traverse delicately to the foot of a discontinuous flake
crack. Climb this for 30ft., passing some wedged flakes, to
the foot of a V-groove which leads more easily to a stance
and thread belay at the left hand end of the long terrace.
4) 85ft. Move up to the left then down round a rib to a
ledge, then make an ascending traverse to a chockstone
belay in Central Chimney.   5) 55ft. Move round to the
right to a ledge below a smooth groove. Climb the right
wall for 10ft. then traverse right again (crux) to reach a
square cut groove. Continue up this and step right to a
ledge and belay.   6) 95ft. The cracked rib on the left is
followed by easier rock to a good stance below a grassy
groove.   7) 50ft. Pleasant climbing up the left wall of the
groove to the top of the crag.

180 **Eagle Front**   ***   VS
495ft.   *W. Peascod and S. B. Beck   1940*
This splendid climb takes a meandering but logical route up
the front of the buttress. In dry conditions the climbing is
pleasant and sustained: in wet conditions the route becomes
a major epic. Starts up a rib about 60ft. left of the corner of
the crag.
1) 60ft. The rib is followed by a short traverse right to a
good belay.   2) 95ft. Climb the groove until it is possible to
traverse right at the earliest opportunity to the foot of a
gangway sloping up to the left. Follow the gangway
(often wet) to a steep groove. This is climbed using sloping
holds on the left wall to a small ledge and good runner.
Move right then back left underneath a bulge onto some
slabs, then follow a line of flakes back right to an overhung
ledge.   3) 60ft. Pull into a shallow groove above the
right-hand end of the ledge, step right and ascend easily to
the Terrace.   4) 75ft. The Terrace is traversed to the left,
passing a small slab using a doubtful undercut flake to a
stance and a small thread belay immediately left of the slab.
Piton belay recommended.   5) 45ft. Move left to a higher
ledge, then climb the steep wall above on awkwardly
spaced holds until a delicate move can be made into an

open groove on the right. This is climbed to a bulge, when a sloping ledge with poor belays is reached by another step right. Piton usually in place.   6) 65ft. Traverse right in a fine position to the foot of a clean slab (often wet). Climb this with difficulty to a ledge and chockstone belay.

7) 60ft. The fine crack in the corner is a great deal easier than its appearance would suggest. Step right at the top to reach a magnificent stance and belay.   8) 35ft. Finish up easy rock.

GREY CRAG   (172148)

This crag lies just to the west of Eagle Crag and, being of south-easterly aspect, is altogether a drier and sunnier place. It consists of four rather broken buttresses of grey rough rock, in ascending altitude Harrow Buttress, Mitre Buttress, Chockstone Buttress, and Oxford and Cambridge Buttress (see photograph). The climbs are shorter and less serious than the routes on Eagle Crag, with more routes in the lower grades. By joining routes on the buttresses a long climb can be made, leading to within 100yds. of the summit of High Stile.

Access: As for Eagle Crag, then climb the scree to the foot of the crag.

Descent: By scree gullies on the left of the crags or heather slopes on the right (east).

181 **Harrow Buttress**   D

130ft.   *W. Bishop and W. A. Woodsend   1912*

A short but popular route. Start just left of the lowest point of the crag. Combined with Rib and Wall, over 400ft. of excellent climbing can be had.

1) 30ft. The arete is climbed on good holds to a belay on the right.   2) 40ft. Continue up the chimney then traverse left to a rock ledge below a broken groove.   3) 60ft. The groove and easy rock lead to an overhung corner. Move left and continue to the top of the buttress. The start of Rib and Wall is 80ft. down the rake on the left.

182 **Mitre Buttress Direct**   *   VD

235ft.   *A. C. Pigou and party   1915*

A rather broken route with one very good pitch up the wall to the right of the cave. Starts at the foot of a subsidiary

75 Grey Crag, Buttermere

buttress below the main buttress. A pleasant way of reaching this point is to climb Harrow Buttress then scramble down the gully on the left.

1) 40ft. Climb the subsidiary buttress with a steep initial wall.   2) 45ft. Climb the wall by an awkward pull-up, then scramble to the right to the foot of the face proper.

3) 70ft. Ascend direct to a ledge and continue to a narrow mantelshelf. Traverse left to the edge of the buttress, then follow a scoop on the left to the foot of the prominent cave.

4) 40ft. Climb the wall on the right of the cave. The wall is exposed and looks extremely blank from below, but after an initial awkward move there are very good holds.

5) 40ft. Traverse left to a steep crack and follow this to the top.

183 **Rib and Wall**   D

290ft.   *W. Peascod and G. G. MacPhee*   *1945*

An obvious rib between Mitre and Harrow Buttresses gives the first pitch of this varied climb. Easily reached from the top of Harrow Buttress.

1) 45ft. The rib is climbed to a recess.   2) 30ft. Continue on good holds to a good block belay.   3) 20ft. Climb the blunt nose above with difficulty to a bridged block which joins the rib to the main face.   4) 45ft. Above is a wall of wedged blocks. Climb these trending rightwards to the foot of a V-groove.   5) 35ft. An awkward move round to the right gives access to a narrow ledge which is traversed until a short ascent can be made into a deep recess.   6) 35ft. The wall and crack on the right.   7) 80ft. Slabs of beautifully rough rock lead to the top.

184 **Slabs West Route**   HS

165ft.   *W. Peascod and A. Barton*   *1942*

This route lies on the slabs, on the left side of Chockstone Buttress, which rise from the scree gully between Harrow Buttress and Chockstone Buttress. The start is at a point some 15ft. left of an obvious rightwards traversing line. The climb is a delightful exercise in technique, with minimal protection.

1) 95ft. Move diagonally right then directly up to a good resting place. Go back leftwards until it is possible to go straight up the slab to a terrace.   2) 70ft. From the pile of blocks climb up to a niche on the left. Step out right and

continue directly to the terrace below Oxford and Cambridge Buttress.

185 Oxford and Cambridge Direct Route * MS

125ft.   *H. V. Reade   1914*

A good continuation to the Slabs West Route. It takes the edge of the Oxford and Cambridge Buttress. Start just right of the arete.

1) 45ft. Climb up to an overhang and step left and up to a rock ledge and good belays.   2) 50ft. A short bulging crack on the left proves awkward. Move right and climb the arete delicately to the top of the crag.

186 Suaviter * MS

135ft.   *W. Peascod and S. B. Beck   1941*

A short but interesting route up the line of a crack which splits the left end of Grey Wall. Grey Wall is the wall of perfect rock on the right side of Chockstone Buttress. Start at a large bollard in a shallow corner below the left end of a long ledge.

1) 20ft. Climb the bollard and the corner until it is possible to move right and climb the face to the ledge.   2) 50ft. From the left end of the ledge, move down and make a delicate traverse across the steep wall to a thin crack in the centre of the slab. Climb the crack to a ledge with doubtful blocks and a higher ledge on the left.   3) 65ft. Climb the ridge above and a 20-ft. chimney to the top.

187 Fortiter * MVS

145ft.   *W. Peascod and S. B. Beck   1941*

15ft. right of Suaviter is a long crack bisecting some small roofs, and this provides the line of this exhilarating little climb.

1) 20ft. Good holds lead to the right-hand end of the long narrow ledge.   2) 70ft. The thin crack in the wall above is started from the right. The crack has good holds until a more awkward move over the overhang can be made. Step right into another crack and up this to a good stance and belay.   3) 55ft. The corner crack and arete above lead to the top.

GREEN CRAG (201131)

This is the recently developed crag at the head of Warnscale Bottom. In general it is heavily vegetated, but it has several climbs of character in the upper grades. The two climbs here described are typical of the crag. Being more popular than the rest they have now become thoroughly defoliated and rank with the best climbs in the area. Unfortunately the crag is very slow to dry.

Approach: The cliff faces north-west and can be reached in ¾ hr. from Gatescarth along the Fleetwith Quarry track. Where this starts to rise from the valley floor, the stream is crossed and a pleasant zig-zag path is followed up the tongue between the streams to the foot of the crag. The cliff can be reached in a slightly longer time from Honister Pass by following the old Drumhouse track over the col. The top of the crag is in an area of rocky knolls, reached by a short descent and crossing the stream.

Descent: To the south of the crag by scrambling down broken ground overlooking the ravine of Black Beck.

188 **Paper Tiger** ** MVS

270ft. *J. A. Austin and N. J. Soper 1966*

The climb makes an impressive ascending traverse into the centre of the crag starting at a holly below the right-hand of two big green corners. This corner is Thorgrim, a wet HVS.

1) 110ft. A short cleaned groove and slab are followed by steep grass which is climbed to a dead tree up to the left, level with the foot of the corner. 2) 80ft. The large overhang 6oft. up to the left is gained by a long ascending traverse (no protection). Climb the overhang, which proves less alarming than appearances would suggest, to a good stance and piton belay. 3) 80ft. The steep wall above is climbed, zig-zagging right or left when difficulties appear, to the top of the crag.

189 **Saraband** ** HVS

275ft. *J. A. Austin and T. Sullivan 1967*

This fine route turns the overhangs to the left of Paper Tiger by slab climbing of great elegance. Start at a deep vegetated groove directly below the left end of the overhangs, and about 6oft. right of a tree-topped pedestal.

1) 25ft. Scramble up the groove to a piton belay. 2) 80ft.

Climb the steep slabs, trending slightly leftwards to a small stance 15ft. below the large overhangs. Peg belay.   3) 110ft. Climb up to the overhang then traverse left into a green groove. This is climbed to a resting place just above a small overhang. Step left to a good foothold on the edge of the slab and climb this on dwindling holds until forced to step round the arete on the left into a groove (often wet). Up this to a stance and piton belay on the left. A sustained pitch.   4) 60ft. Easy rocks to the top.

HIGH CRAG   (183145)

The rocky northern face of High Crag steepens directly above Gatescarth farm into a steep pillar of sound clean rhyolite which yields several good routes.
Approach: Either directly up the hillside or, longer but less laboriously, by following the Birkness Combe track to the old wall at the entrance to the combe, then striking back leftwards to the foot of the crag.
Descent: Well to the left (east).

190 **Samson**   HVS
230ft. *O. Woolcock and R. D. Brown   1964*
Ascends the steep, smooth wall on the east side of the main buttress. A magnificent second pitch. Start on the Rock Table Ledge—a little way up on the left.
1) 70ft. From the blocks follow a rib on the right then grass to a large ledge.   2) 110ft. Make an ascending traverse right above the overhang to gain the thin crack in the centre of the wall. Piton runner. The crack is climbed with difficulty to easier ground. Continue to a block belay.
3) 50ft. Easy slabs to the top.

191 **High Crag Buttress**   **   HVS
190ft. *L. Kendal and R. McHaffie   1963*
A short but very fine route, of a high standard of difficulty and on perfect rock. The climb commences directly below the crack line which passes between a pair of prominent niches or 'eyes'.

76 *Overleaf left: High Crag, Buttermere*

77 *Overleaf right: Samson, High Crag*

1) 15ft. Easy climbing to an ash. 2) 40ft. Climb onto a pedestal behind the ash and continue up the crack above to the left-hand cave. 3) 50ft. Climb the overhang between the caves and continue up the fine chimney to another niche and chockstone belay. 4) 80ft. Climb the right-hand arete to a good thread runner, then make an extremely delicate ascending traverse to gain an easier-angled area up to the right. The groove above leads without further difficulty to the top.

192 **Delilah**   *   MVS
165ft.   *W. Peascod and B. Blake   1951*
Follows a fine groove up the right-hand side of the buttress. Start just left of the foot of the chimney bounding the buttress on the right-hand side.
1) 55ft. Gain a higher ledge, then move up to a narrow rock ledge. Traverse right and climb a thin crack to a stance and belay. 2) 110ft. Climb up and left into the groove, which is followed directly to the top.

DALE HEAD CRAG   (225156)
This cliff is finely situated at the head of Newlands Valley on the north face of the fell of the same name. The rock is good but rather vegetated and slow to dry.
Approach: From Honister Pass, the Dale Head path leads off directly northwards to Dale Head Tarn. Pass to the left of the tarn, contour the northern flank of the fell and trend downwards to pass below a rock rib. The crag is then reached up a steep scree slope (approximately $\frac{3}{4}$ hr.).
Descent: Cross the knife-edge then descend a gully on the right.

193 **Dale Head Pillar**   MVS
260ft.   *W. Peascod and G. Rushworth   1948*
A classic climb, steep and exposed in the upper section. Start just right of the Pillar, which is itself on the left of the main face. Scramble 15ft. to a grassy corner below a crack.
1) 80ft. Follow the crack to a ledge and belay. 2) 40ft. Climb the wall on the left of a grassy groove, until a traverse left can be made to a large ledge on top of the

78 Mithril, Dale Head Crag

Pillar.   3) 6oft. Ascend the steep and exposed groove on
the right. Exit on the left and climb a slab to a recess and
thread belay.   4) 8oft. A short wall leads to a ledge;
then climb a bulging wall starting on the right. An open
groove and easier climbing leads to the top.

194 **Mithril**   **   HVS
300ft. *N. J. Soper and A. Wright 1963*
An impressive climb for its standard. The start is at a
rightward-facing cracked groove, about 25yds. right of the
corner of the crag.
1) 55ft. Climb the crack and step left into a shallow groove.
Move up to a grass terrace.   2) 7oft. Above are two
grooves. Enter the left one and climb it and the left arete
until a leftward traverse can be made to a crack. Climb this
to a forbidding recess. Good belays.   3) 5oft. Climb the
overhanging crack to gain an overhung gangway on the
right. Follow this and make an exposed move over the
bulge into a niche. Peg belay.   4) 65ft. Traverse left
below another overhang to gain easier grooves leading to
an iron spike. Belay.   5) 6oft. Easy rocks lead to the crest
of the crag.

MINERS' CRAG   (232158)

This pleasant and unfrequented crag lies on the east side of
the head of Newlands valley conveniently opposite Dale
Head Crag. It faces south-west and dries quite quickly, so is
a useful alternative to Buckstone Howe and the Borrowdale
Crags.
Approach: The quickest approach is usually from the top of
Honister, as for Dale Head Pillar, but keeping to the right
side of Newlands Beck. Alternatively, cars can be driven up
the valley from Little Town as far as Castle Nook. Follow
the good track until level with Dale Head Pillar. Miners'
Crag is the last crag on the left.
Topography: The lowest section of the crag is a flat buttress
between a gully on the left (Newlands Gully, VD) and
broken ground on the right. Higher up on the right is a
series of steep slabby grooves and ribs, giving the climbs
described below, and ending on the Quartz Rake. Above
and to the right is another steep but shorter wall.
Descent: The climbs described below finish on the Quartz

Rake. Descend this to the right.

195 **Miners' Grooves** * MVS

245ft. *G. Rushworth, W. Peascod and G. G. MacPhee* *1948*

A good groove climb, well protected but with some suspect rock in the upper section. Starts at a slab below a steep V-groove, near the left end of the south-west face.

1) 40ft. Easy slabs lead to the foot of the groove. 2) 90ft. Ascend the groove for 45ft. to a stance below the steep upper section. Swing left on a good hold to the arete, then climb the arete and the shallow gully above to a belay.
3) 55ft. Climb the main groove in the wall above. Belays on the right. 4) 60ft. Easy but loose ribs lead to the Quartz Rake.

196 **Corkscrew** HS

210ft. *G. Rushworth and W. Dennison* *1948*

A good route up the slabs and ribs to the right of Miners' Grooves. Starts 30ft. to the right of that climb, below the left end of a prominent slab.

1) 50ft. Climb a rib to a niche at the left edge of the slab. Belays up on the left. 2) 80ft. Ascend a steep little crack on the left, and continue up the groove above. Traverse right into another groove and climb this to an exposed stance. Move back left across the top of the groove and go up easily to a stance and spike belays below a sweep of slabs and a steep corner above. 3) 80ft. Cross the slabs to the ridge on the right. Climb the airy exposed arete, the hardest part of the climb, then the easier ridge above to the Quartz Rake.

WINTER CLIMBING

Much of the Buttermere and Newlands area is too low and near the sea for good winter climbing. Birkness Combe can offer a variety of winter routes; Birkness Chimney and Birkness Gully give excellent climbs with a broken region of crags and gullies to the east offering easier routes. Central Chimney on Eagle Crag could give a superb and difficult winter climb. In a hard winter the north-facing gullies in Warnscale Bottom occasionally come into condition and give difficult climbs. Finally, Grasmoor has a large crag in its northern combe

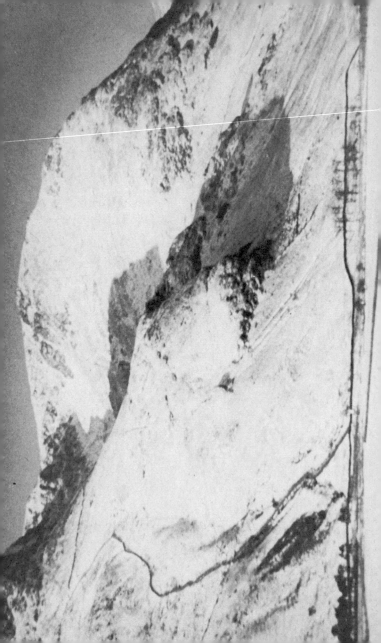

(Dove Crag—179204). This is reached in about 1½ hours from Lanthwaite Green. There are three gullies giving good and often hard climbs.

When the Buttermere crags are out of condition it is worth remembering that Gable Crag is usually better and only an hour's walk from the top of Honister Pass (see Wasdale section).

79 *Buttermere in winter. High Crag, Eagle Crag and Grey Crag are visible in Birkness Combe*

The main attraction of this quiet afforested valley is the towering bastion of Pillar Rock, a unique geological feature which inspired the beginnings of the sport of rock-climbing in Lakeland. The crag offers a wide variety of excellent routes at all standards of difficulty, with the added attraction that the climbs are not usually crowded. In bad weather, however, the Rock becomes very greasy, and even routes of Difficult standard can become major epics. At a lower altitude, pleasant climbing can be found on the crags on Bowness Knot (111155) and on Anglers' Crag (099151). There is a public car-park at the foot of Bowness Knott, at the start of the Forestry Commission road. The upper part of the valley is shown on the Buttermere map.

Access

The entrance to the valley is conveniently reached by road from Cockermouth, Whitehaven and Calder Bridge. Unfortunately for the climber, the Forestry Commission has imposed a ban on unauthorised vehicles using the unmetalled road which runs up the valley from the car park at Bowness Knott. An agreement between the Forestry Commission and the British Mountaineering Council allows a limited number of vehicles to drive as far as Gillerthwaite. The procedure is:—   1) collect a numbered permit from either Colin Warnham, Dower Cottage, Pardshaw Hall, Cockermouth, tel. Cockermouth 3531, or Peter Moffat, Cross Lanes, Seascale, tel. Seascale 230;   2) inform the Head Forester, tel. Lamplugh 275, before using the road;   3) display the permit and park in the car park at Gillerthwaite. The valley can also be reached by long but pleasant walks:

a) from Wasdale via Black Sail Pass
b) from Buttermere over Scarth Gap Pass
c) from Borrowdale—from the top of Honister Pass via a good track leading first west, then south-west over the slopes of Brandreth to the head of Ennerdale.

The nearest public transport to the valley is an infrequent bus service to Ennerdale Bridge from Whitehaven.

Accommodation and Camping

Accommodation in Ennerdale is sparse: incredibly, the Anglers' Hotel was demolished to allow the level of the lake to be raised—a plan which has now been shelved! Several of the farms at the lower end of the valley and around

Ennerdale Bridge offer accommodation and will allow camping
There are two Youth Hostels in the valley: the famous
Black Sail (194123) hostel at the head of the valley, and
another at Gillerthwaite (142141) near the head of the lake.

The variety of insect life in the Ennerdale forest is an
active discouragement to low-level bivouacs, but high
camp-sites and fair-weather bivouacs can be found below
Pillar Rock.

Food and Drink

Many of the farmhouses in the region serve excellent teas,
and there is a café in Ennerdale Bridge. The nearest
restaurants are in Cleator Moor and Whitehaven.
Fortunately, there is a pleasant pub in Ennerdale Bridge,
the Fox and Hounds, which serves bar snacks as well as Lion
Licensing hours are 11.30–2.30 pm and 5.30–10.30 pm
on weekdays and 12–2 pm and 7–10.30 pm on Sundays,
with 11 pm closing on Fridays and Saturdays. There are
two small shops in Ennerdale Bridge and larger stores in
Cleator Moor and Whitehaven (early closing day
Wednesday).

Garages and Car Hire

Petrol can be bought in Ennerdale Bridge. There are
service stations in Cleator Moor and Whitehaven, and the
nearest AA garage is at Cockermouth, tel. 3391. Car hire in
Whitehaven, tel. 2697 or 2311.

General Services

There is a public telephone in Ennerdale Bridge; there are
also public toilets there. The nearest mountaineering shops
are in Whitehaven and at Wasdale Head.

Mountain Rescue

There is a mountain rescue post at Ennerdale Youth
Hostel, Gillerthwaite (142141), tel. Lamplugh 237, and an
unmanned post (172124) at the foot of Shamrock, Pillar
Rock (40yds. east of the foot of Walker's Gully). There is
also a first aid post at Black Sail Youth Hostel (G.S.
stretcher, Hostel open Easter–31 October only, no telephone,
grid ref. 195123). Otherwise phone 999 as usual.

80 Pillar Rock, from the foot of the firebreak

PILLAR ROCK   (172123)

This superb crag has a number of long and excellent routes
of all grades of difficulty. The rock is sound and gives good
friction in dry conditions, but in wet weather the altitude
and aspect of the crag produce a greasy coating which can
increase the severity of the climbs considerably. In high
summer the north-east face of the Rock catches the early
morning sun and can dry fairly quickly, whereas the west
faces will generally dry in the afternoon.

Approach: The shortest approach to the Rock is still from
Ennerdale, despite the recent restrictions on the use of Forestry
Commission roads. Obtain a permit as explained in the section
on access, then drive to Gillerthwaite. Walk up the road for
about 1½ miles then take a right fork to reach a bridge across
the Liza (165135). Turn left after the bridge and after about
100 yards a sign marking the start of the path to the Rock will
be seen. This leads diagonally through the trees to the combe
below the Rock. Total time to the foot of the Rock about 1½
hours. The approach from Wasdale Head is a long but pleasant
walk (2 hours). From the Wasdale Head Hotel follow the well-
marked path to Black Sail Pass until just after crossing Gather-
stone Beck a path branches left up to the ridge. Follow the ridge
towards Pillar until, just at the start of the steep part, a good
path on the right (cairn) leads round the north-east flank of the
mountain. This is the famous High Level Traverse and leads to
Robinson's Cairn and the east side of the Rock.

From Borrowdale it is possible to start from the top of
Honister Pass and traverse the slopes of Brandreth, then
follow a path below Gable Crag and Kirkfell to the top of
Black Sail. A long walk—about 3 hours to the Rock.
From Buttermere, ascend Scarth Gap Pass then traverse
right for ¼ mile and descend a diagonal path through the
forest. This leads to the river Liza at the new footbridge
and a path ascending to the Rock. About 2 hours.

Topographical: The structure of Pillar Rock is somewhat
complicated, and deserves some study in advance. Descent
routes are not straightforward, and many seemingly obvious
descents lead to vertical gullies. *In mist or bad weather
getting off the Rock safely can take considerable skill and
experience:* more parties have been forced to bivouac on

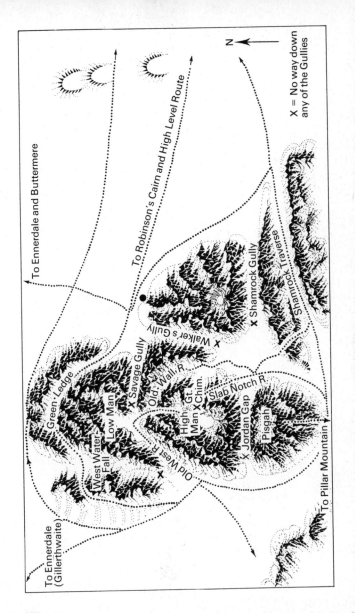

To Ennerdale and Buttermere

To Robinson's Cairn and High Level Route

N

X = No way down any of the Gullies

Green Ledge

West Water Fall

Low Man

X Savage Gully

Old Wall R.

Old West R.

High Gt. Man X Chim.

Slab Notch R.

X Jordan Gap

Pisgah

X Walker's Gully

X Shamrock Gully

Shamrock Traverse

To Ennerdale (Gillerthwaite)

To Pillar Mountain

Pillar than on any other crag in Lakeland.

A plan of the Rock is given on page 215. The crag is conical in appearance, the top being named High Man, whilst a subsidiary shoulder on the valley side is called Low Man. The south side of the Rock is short and separated from the main mass of Pillar Mountain by a rift (Jordan Gap) and a subsidiary peak known as Pisgah. The north and west faces of the Rock are long and give the best climbing. At the corner of the north and west faces is a deep gully, the Waterfall, and above lies the West Cove. The east edge of the Waterfall gives a polished route of moderate standard (harder when wet), whilst the buttress on the right gives easy scrambling except for a 20ft. chimney near its foot. Along the base of the North Face is a large terrace, the Green Ledge, and below this is a subsidiary belt of slabs. To the east of the North Face lies the buttress of Shamrock, separated from the Rock by the famous cleft of Walker's Gully. The north-east face of Shamrock is split by Shamrock Gully (VS). High up the north-east side of Shamrock is a wide rock ledge, the Shamrock Traverse. This provides an easy route to the south and west faces of the Rock from Robinson's Cairn. Follow the traverse then go behind Pisgah and down scree to the west faces. The Shamrock Traverse also provides an excellent descent route, although note that the traverse lies *above* the top of Shamrock Gully and care should be taken not to confuse the two in descent.

SHAMROCK

Shamrock is the first part of the crag to be reached on the approach from Wasdale, and a prominent landmark is the blue stretcher box at its base. The main part of the crag is split by a diagonal ramp, the Great Heather Shelf, rising from left to right. Because of this and other large ledges the climbs are more broken than elsewhere on Pillar, but the individual pitches are as good as any on the Rock. Photon, Eros and Thanatos are the quickest routes to dry after rain. *Descent:* From the Tea-Table block at the top of Shamrock, scramble down for some 30ft. to the col at the top of

81 Pillar Rock, The Shamrock
GHS = Great Heather Shelf

Shamrock Gully. Do NOT attempt to descend this, but scramble up the grassy gully on the right for 150ft. to gain the Shamrock Traverse footpath. Follow this leftwards off the crag.

197 **Photon**   MVS

490ft.   *W. A. Barnes and party   1967*

A long route with varied climbing, well protected and with large stances. The rock is clean and the climb dries relatively quickly as it catches the early morning sun. Start at the foot of the obvious cleaned groove reached by scrambling up the left side of the Great Heather Shelf for 200ft.

1) 80ft. Climb the groove to a ledge. Piton belay.   2) 100ft. Move right and climb the slabby corner to where the groove steepens. Climb the corner to below a bulge. Fix protection in the crack on the right, then climb this by a layback move. Continue up the crack to reach a good ledge on the left.   3) 40ft. Climb the corner formed by a large chockstone, then move right to a grassy bay.   4) 100ft. Climb straight up the pleasant slab on the left to a ledge overlooking Shamrock Gully, below the final square tower. Scramble up to the left for 20ft. to a belay on the edge of the gully. It is possible to escape from this point up the easy upper section of Shamrock Gully.   5) 70ft. The open groove on the left of the tower is climbed, passing a block, to the crest of the ridge above the tower. 15ft. above is another ledge and belay. Alternatively take the groove on the left, immediately above the belay: steeper and more strenuous but with better protection.   6) 100ft. Easier scrambling along the Alpine-style ridge leads to the Tea-Table block at the top of Shamrock.

198 **Eros**   *   XS

290ft.   *W. S. Lounds and J. C. Eilbeck   1968*

A series of eliminate variations on Photon giving good sustained climbing with little protection. Starts as for Photon, or, better, by climbing Thanatos and walking left across the Great Heather Shelf.

1) 80ft. Climb the rib on the right of the cleaned groove. The final 20ft. is very delicate, up the centre of a mossy triangular slab with an awkward grassy landing. Piton belay as for Photon.   2) 110ft. Climb the steep rib directly above,

to the left of the slabby groove of Photon. The angle eases at 60ft., but the slab above is still delicate and unprotected. Finally a ledge is reached and a traverse can be made to the left to a grassy bay and belay.   3) 100ft. The overhanging groove above is the next obstacle. The blank middle section has been climbed free, but most parties will be forced onto the steep bounding rib on the right. Continue to a ledge above (belay). Step back left across the groove and climb the left edge of the slab and the broken rib above to join Photon at the top of pitch 4 of that climb.

199 **Thanatos/Electron**   **   HVS/VS
535ft. *J. C. Eilbeck and W. S. Lounds   1968*
A. G. Cram and J. C. Eilbeck   1966
A very good combination, sustained at VS standard with the crux of Thanatos being slightly harder. Thanatos can be avoided if necessary by scrambling up the left side of the Great Heather Shelf (which splits the two climbs) for 200ft. to the foot of an obvious corner some 70ft. right of Photon. Electron dries rather slowly after heavy rain. Start 20ft. right of the conspicuous blue stretcher box at the bottom of Shamrock, below the big corner capped by two overhangs.
1) 8oft. Climb a slab and up to a corner. Ascend this, with an exit on the slab on the left, and continue up bilberry ledges to a belay beneath the corner proper.   2) 100ft. Climb the corner (the right-hand of two grooves) to the large overhang. Traverse left round the rib into the second groove and bridge up this until the good ledge on the left can be gained (crux).   3) 20ft. of climbing. The easy corner above leads to the Great Heather Shelf. Scramble across this, slightly down to the left, to the bottom of a big corner which is the first pitch of Electron.   4) 85ft. Climb onto the higher grass ledge and continue up the square corner. A bulge proves awkward at mid-height and further up another problematical move is overcome before the holds improve and a good grass ledge is reached.   5) 8oft. Continue up the groove for 40ft., then go right across a ledge to a short wall which leads to a large block belay below and to the left of a fine layback crack.   6) 70ft.

A good pitch. Climb the crack to a resting place and good runner at 40ft. Continue up the final steeper section to a belay on the slab above. 7) 100ft. The difficulties and angle now relent. Climb the grey arete above, move right and follow a second arete to the Tea Table block at the top of Shamrock.

200 **Shamrock Tower** * MVS
550ft. *S. H. Cross and party 1940*
A classic mountaineering route despite the large field at mid-height. The rock is good but becomes very greasy in the wet. Starts 20ft. right of the stretcher box at the foot of Shamrock.
1) 60ft. Climb an easy-angled cleaned slab and scramble up a few feet to the foot of a corner. Follow this for a few feet until it is possible to break out left up a steep slab to a ledge. Belay on another ledge a few feet higher. 2) 70ft. Step round the rib on the right and ascend steeply for 20ft. Traverse right and climb a small awkward corner to a ledge and large block belay. 3) 80ft. Traverse left from the block and balance into a V-groove. Climb this, moving right, and then go up diagonally on the right to grass. Move back left to a block belay. 4) 130ft. Move right and ascend grooves to the Great Heather Shelf. Cross this diagonally to the right to a large flake belay. 5) 30ft. Ascend a few feet, then traverse right to a sitting belay. 6) 120ft. Climb the corner on the right for 20ft, then move right to gain the long corner, which gives very pleasant crack and chimney climbing. At the top exit right to a belay. 7) 60ft. Continue up the easier broken ridge above to the top of Shamrock.

201 **Walker's Gully** *** HS
390ft. *O. G. Jones, G. D. Abraham and A. E. Field 1899*
One of the most famous of the classic gullies. Start at the foot of the deep cleft between Shamrock and the North Face of Low Man. There is some danger of stonefall if there are parties on the scree fan above the gully.
1) 50ft. An easy pitch, then scree to the foot of a high, green chimney. 2) 30ft. The right wall of the chimney to a belay. 3) 40ft. An exposed groove with poor holds

82 The long corner of Electron, Pillar Rock

leads past the first chockstone. 4) 8oft. Scrambling up the gully bed. 5) 3oft. Rocks on the left to a wet cave. 6) 3oft. Climb up behind, then over the first chockstone. Bridge the gully to a sloping chockstone then gain good holds over the upper chockstone. 7) 3oft. Easy ground to a cave with a window. 8) 15ft. A strenuous struggle through the hole. 9) 55ft. An easy through-route or a staircase on the right leads to big boulders. Go over these to a cave below the huge capstone of the gully. 10) 3oft. Move across the right wall on sloping holds. A tall man can then back-up with his back on the left wall. Otherwise continue rather strenuously up the right wall to the Amphitheatre.

NORTH FACE OF LOW MAN

This fine face gives some of the longest and most exposed routes on the Rock. All the routes start from the Green Ledge, though some pitches on the slabs below can be found. Grooved Wall is the only route hereabouts which dries quickly. A good combination is to start with a route here and continue up the West Face of High Man—a total of about 700ft. of climbing.

Descent: It is best either to continue up well-scratched rocks to High Man and descend from there, or to descend the Old West Route: from the top of Low Man traverse round to the right (west) on a good path which becomes an easy scramble and leads diagonally to the West Cove. It is possible to traverse east to the top of Walker's Gully, but as this route is rather loose it is not recommended.

202 **Grooved Wall** ** VS

28oft. *H. M. Kelly, H. G. Knight and W. G. Standring 1928*
An excellent route taking a series of grooves up the right (true left) wall of Walker's Gully. Start just to the right of the gully, 5oft. of scrambling above the path.

1) 6oft. Climb awkward grassy ledges to a wide chimney, which leads to the top of a large flake. 2) 3oft. Ascend the groove above to a ledge on the right. 3) 6oft. The

83 *Pillar Rock, North Face*
GL = Green Ledge. 201 = Walker's Gully. ST = Shamrock Traverse

groove above is barred by an overhang which forms the hardest part of the climb. Fortunately some good protection can be arranged in the crack leading over the overhang. Continue up the groove to a belay. 4) 6oft. After some initial steepness the angle eases and the groove is followed to a ledge and belay. 5) 7oft. The final groove is not easy. Above the groove some ledges lead to a stance and belay. Scramble up until the scree on the left can be gained above Walker's Gully, taking care not to bombard possible parties below. The Shamrock Traverse lies about 3ooft. above.

203 **North-east Climb** * HVD
420ft. *G. D. and A. P. Abraham 1912*
A fine climb which becomes considerably harder in wet or greasy conditions. Start as for the North Climb.
1) 100ft. The first pitch of the North Climb (q.v.). Then climb 65ft. up the second pitch to belay above a chimney.
2) 30ft. Move a few feet up the gully then traverse across the rib on the left. A 10ft. chimney leads to a small stance and belay. 3) 25ft. Move left round the rib then across a slab to grassy ledges. 4) 35ft. Two chimneys with a difficult finish. 5) 40ft. Climb a short slab on the left then walk left to the foot of a long V-groove on the wall of Walker's Gully. 6) 8oft. Ascend the groove. 7) 6oft. A mossy wall on the right then a vertical chimney and easier rocks. 8) 5oft. A steep chimney and grassy ledges lead to the top. From here traverse, with care, either left to the amphitheatre above Walker's Gully or right to Low Man.

204 **North Climb** ** HD
320ft. *W. P. Haskett-Smith, G. Hastings and W. C. Slingsby 1891*
A popular classic, with good belays and short pitches making the climb suitable for large parties. The final pitch is Mild Severe unless the alternative finish, involving an abseil, is taken. In wet weather the polished nature of the holds makes the climbing somewhat harder. Starts at the left hand end of Green Ledge, at a short wall below a large ledge.
1) 35ft. An easy mantelshelf and a slab trending left lead to a ledge at the foot of an obvious gully line (Savage Gully).

84 Looking down the last pitch of Grooved Wall, Pillar Rock

2) 95ft. Climb the line of the gully for three short pitches to the foot of a deep twisting chimney on the right. At this point the gully steepens and twists to the left.   3) 40ft. Squirm up the twisting chimney to a good ledge and belay. 4) 45ft. Climb the open V-chimney slanting up to the left, then move right to a good ledge.   5) 45ft. On the right wall of the corner above is a slanting chimney crack (the 'Stomach Traverse'). Climb this to a large ledge.   6) 20ft. Climb the cave pitch in the corner. Above this a short walk leads to the massive 'Split Blocks'.   7) 20ft. Climb the chimney between the blocks to their top.   8) 20ft. Traverse to the left to a good ledge below and to the right of the projecting Nose. The first few feet (the Strid) are awkward and exposed.   9) 25ft. The Nose (MS). From the corner on the right-hand side of the Nose traverse out on a good flake foothold. At this point a good side hold for the left hand can be reached, and by pulling on this and using a hidden foot (or knee!) hold round the corner the Nose can be surmounted. From the top of the Nose an easy (but loose) gully leads to the top of Low Man.

Alternative finishes: 9a) 25ft. The Hand Traverse (HS). From the right end of the ledge ascend the steep wall for 10ft. until a good flake can be reached. Hand traverse to the left to gain the top of the Nose. 9b) 130ft. Descent into Savage Gully (HD). From the ledge below the Nose, abseil down on the left into Savage Gully and traverse to the left, round the corner, to the foot of a V-chimney. Climb the chimney without difficulty, then traverse up to the right for 60ft. to the ledges above the Nose.

205 **Scylla**   *   VS
44ft.   *A. G. Cram and W. Young   1963*
The climb takes the impressive crack splitting the large wall set in the centre of the north face. Unfortunately the introductory pitches are rather scrappy, but the main pitches give excellent sustained climbing at the upper limit of its grade. The obvious Direct Finish is XS. Starts in a small grassy bay to the left of the Nor'-nor'-west Climb, directly below the obvious crack pitch high above.
1) 90ft. Scramble up into a corner. Climb the corner on the right, then move right and scramble up ledges and over a large boulder to the foot of a wide square chimney.
2) 90ft. The chimney is awkward to start, but soon relents

228

and leads to a large ledge. Continue up in the same line, or move left and climb a groove, to reach the foot of a steep wall. Belay on the left.   3) 110ft. Climb the fine crack splitting the wall. The first 40ft. are the hardest, but frequent runners and good jams help to relieve the tension. At the top, pull out left to a good ledge. Large but dubious block belays or a piton.   4) 90ft. Climb the steep wall behind the belay until the right-hand end of a horizontal break can be reached. Make a long stride to the left and pull round onto a ledge with difficulty. Continue traversing round to the left with an awkward balance move at the end to reach a V-groove. Jam up the groove until the top of the pinnacle which forms its left side can be reached. Cross the steep wall on the right and pull round to easy ground. Scramble up to a stance and belay.
5) 60ft. Easier but looser climbing on the right leads to the summit of Low Man.

206 **Puppet**   *   XS
440ft.   *A. G. Cram and B. Whybrow*   *1966*
An alternative way up the large wall taken by the crack of Scylla. The climbing becomes better and harder as height is gained, pitch 5 being particularly exposed and exciting. The start and the first two pitches to the foot of the steep wall are the same as those given for Scylla (q.v.).   3) 60ft. Ascend the crack of Scylla for 20ft. to a good runner. Traverse right across the wall (steep and delicate) to the foot of a deep groove. Climb the groove or the arete on the right to a small stance and belay.   4) 60ft. Take the corner and vague rib above until a few moves right lead to a small stance below the steep wall above. Piton belay.
5) 70ft. Climb the steep shallow groove above, and continue up the impending wall above on widely spaced holds, which improve, to a good ledge.   6) 80ft. Move left and climb easier rocks to the top of Low Man.

207 **Nor'-nor'-west Climb**   **   VS
450ft.   *A. T. Hargreaves and G. G. Macphee*   *1932*
The upper half is particularly fine and exposed. A delicate and classic climb. Start at the right-hand side of a large grassy bay in the corner under the bounding buttress.
1) 100ft. After the initial slab, trend away from the wall for 40ft., then back towards a wide crack.   2) 30ft. Climb

up to a large block and turn it on the left.   3) 40ft. Up the slab trending left to a ledge. Climb the corner on the right to the large ledge on top of the buttress (junction with N.W. Climb).   4) 30ft. A V-groove just left of the glacis. 5) 50ft. An exposed traverse left, slightly down at first, crosses the top of a crack near the finish and ends on a sloping ledge and belay.   6) 60ft. Climb up for some 15ft. then move onto the exposed arete on the left. Ascend this to the overhang where a few moves right lead to a small stance and peg belay.   7) 35ft. Traverse right to small ledges.   8) 55ft. Climb a 10ft. crack on the left, then follow a ledge up and leftwards to a belay.   9) 50ft. The arete on the left leads to the summit.

208 **North-west Climb**   ***   MVS
445ft.   *F. W. Botterill and party   1906*
A fine climb on clean rock, enjoyable even in wet weather. Starts at the right-hand end of Green Ledge below a short gangway leading to the right.
1) 70ft. Climb the gangway to a ledge, then a 30ft. chimney followed by a traverse across a slab on the left.   2) 55ft. A chimney leads to a corner and belay.   3) 50ft. Ascend the short buttress on the left, then a crack to easier ground. Go right across the large platform to a large easy-angled slab.   4) 30ft. Climb the slab and a corner, then traverse left to a belay.   5) 60ft. Traverse round a corner on the left, then ascend a bulge and two ledges to reach a recess. Leave this on the right with an awkward move to reach a grass ledge. Continue up to a higher ledge and belay.
6) 20ft. Climb the corner, then left to a delicate nose of rock which leads to Block Ledge.   7) 80ft. Step left and ascend ledges to a short V-chimney. Bridge up the chimney, then make a long stride back across the top of the chimney and climb mossy rock with poor holds to some small grassy ledges.   8) 20ft. Traverse right and climb to the foot of a steep chimney. Good belay but poor stance.   9) 60ft. Oppenheimer's Chimney. The start is hard but protected by a good runner. At the top of the chimney 20ft. of scrambling lead to the summit of Low Man.

209 **Charybdis**   **   HVS
435ft.   *A. G. Cram and W. Young   1964*
The route follows a series of imposing cracks and grooves

up the north-west arete. Start from Green Ledge as for the North-west Climb.

1) 50ft. Climb the gangway and the 30ft. chimney.

2) 100ft. Continue up the same chimney then climb a wall split by cracks to a large platform. 3) 70ft. Move right to a glacis. Climb this and the corner above to belay below the deep, overhanging groove. 4) 50ft. Climb into the groove (runner). Move down onto the left wall and ascend a layback flake. Return to the groove along an awkward gangway and move up to a sloping stance and thread belay.

5) 40ft. Climb the green groove above. Move left at the top to a stance and belay. 6) 50ft. The groove on the right (or the fine arete on the right of the groove) to a large block belay. 7) 75ft. Climb the shallow groove above (20ft. right of Oppenheimer's Chimney). Move right over the bulge then follow a slanting crack up the wall to the top.

WEST FACE OF LOW MAN

This wall of excellent, clean rock catches the afternoon sun and offers relatively short climbs in the lower grades. They can however be followed by a route on the West Face of High Man, after a short descent down the Old West Route.

Descent: At the top of the climbs traverse right to reach a good path (the Old West Route) which becomes an easy scramble and leads diagonally down to the West Cove.

210 **The Appian Way**   **   HS
215ft.   *H. M. Kelly and R. E. W. Pritchard   1923*

A particularly fine wall climb with impressive situations. Start by a large block on a terrace reached by scrambling across from the chockstone at the head of the waterfall.

1) 60ft. Climb up on the left of a mossy chimney for 15ft. then step back right across the corner. Continue up the corner to a stance and flake belay. 2) 50ft. Climb the thin crack in the corner and at the top traverse delicately across the wall on the left to a fine, airy spike for a belay.

3) 40ft. Move left and ascend a series of steep ledges to a grass ledge with a large block leaning against the wall. Thread and spike belays. 4) 70ft. Ascend the impending crack on the left of the block and continue up slabs to the top.

85 *left: Pitch 6 of Charybdis, Pillar Rock*

86 *above: Pillar Rock, West Face of Low Man*
 OW = Old West Route

2 10ft. *H. M. Kelly and party* *1919*

A pleasant climb on good clean rock. Good belays are
frequent, and all the pitches given below can be split if
desired. Starts 40ft. above the chockstone at the top of the
waterfall.

1) 30ft. Climb a mantelshelf to a ledge, then ascend a
V-shaped chimney. Belay on the left. 2) 50ft. Straight up
steeply to a sloping ledge, then a short traverse right
followed by more steep climbing to a glacis. Belay in the
corner. 3) 60ft. The crack on the right wall is followed to
a good ledge. Traverse up to the left for 40ft. to a pile of
blocks. 4) 70ft. Climb the blocks to a good stance and
belay. Continue up a short exposed groove, then easier
climbing leads to the Old West Traverse near the top of
Low Man.

WEST FACE OF HIGH MAN

A superb face which catches the afternoon sun, and gives a
variety of sustained routes on excellent rock. There are
several good slab climbs which are among the first on the
Rock to dry after rain.

Descent: A tricky problem on the first occasion! The best
descent from the top of High Man is to descend the *Slab
and Notch Climb* (Moderate). A few yards north of the
summit cairn, a wide chimney descends on the east side
(right). Descend this for 20ft., then descend well-scratched
slabs on the right (looking out) for some 50ft. until an easy
traverse right leads to the Notch. Descend a short polished
corner, then cross the huge slab to the final short step
leading into the Amphitheatre. (NB—It is necessary to
climb *up* the Amphitheatre to reach either the Shamrock
Traverse or the scree gully leading back to the foot of the
West Face. The scree slopes of the Amphitheatre lead down
into Walker's Gully—HS). An alternative descent is to
abseil or climb down the crack (Difficult) below the summit
to Jordan Gap. Then descend slightly to the east to gain the
Amphitheatre.

The descent on well-scratched rocks to Low Man is graded

87 Appian Way, Pillar Rock

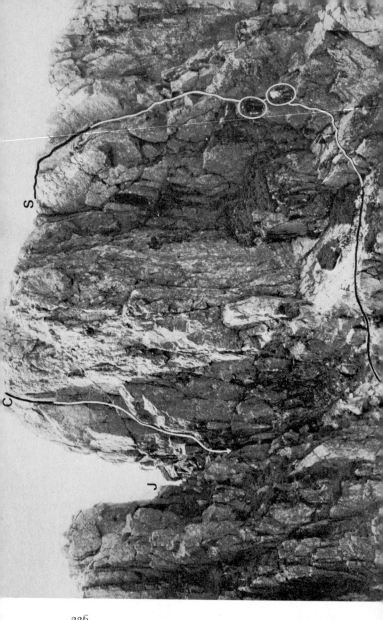

Moderate. This could then be followed by the Old West descent.

212 **Gondor** * XS
250ft.   *A. G. Cram and K. Robson   1967*
The climb takes an improbable line up the bulging arete to the left of the prominent groove of Gomorrah. Probably the most technically difficult climb on the Rock, but difficulties are well-protected. Starts as for Gomorrah.
1) 100ft. As for Gomorrah, the relatively easy lower section of the ridge to a ledge and belay below a steep groove.
2) 60ft. Climb the groove in the arete to a bulge. Move out right across the steep slab to a good foothold. Climb the square-cut overhang above using a sling (in place). Continue up the steep wall above with difficulty to a small stance and piton belay.   3) 90ft. Two alternatives are available to start the pitch. The first possibility is to climb the overhanging arete on the right above the belay for 8ft., using hidden holds round the corner, then move right onto the wall. The second way is to descend slightly, traverse right round the corner, and ascend the steep wall directly. The second possibility is perhaps more difficult but has the advantage that it is possible to see the holds (if the light is good!). From the centre of the wall zig-zag left then continue up the centre to an easier groove. Climb this to a large ledge and belay.

213 **Gomorrah** ** VS
285ft.   *H. M. Kelly and C. F. Holland   1919*
A fine climb taking the big groove on the left side of the face. The route is well-protected and of a reasonable standard if the normal finish is taken. Starts some 70ft. along the Old West Route, 20ft. left of the grassy groove which terminates in a prominent large triangular overhang.
1) 100ft. Follow the line of the ridge above, passing a grass ledge at 35ft., to a ledge and belay below the steep

88 East side of Pillar Rock, from the Amphitheatre, showing Jordan Gap (J) and the descent routes
S = Slab and Notch (Moderate)
C = Central Jordan Climb (Difficult)

buttress on the left of the big groove. 2) 80ft. Move right and slightly down across a slab into the bay beneath the groove. Gain a wide crack on the right which becomes the groove higher up. Climb the groove to a stance on some cracked blocks below a roof. Nut belay. The variation finish goes left from here. 3) 55ft. Climb the steep slabby wall forming the left side of the groove, past the roof, to where the groove steepens. Step into the crack and climb this for 20ft. Traverse out right to a small stance and belay on the rib. 5) 50ft. Return to the chimney and climb this, or more pleasantly take the rib behind the belay: both lead to the top of High Man.

Alternative finish: Take the upper half of the buttress to the left of the final groove. Harder than the original route, giving sustained climbing in superb positions.

3a) 70ft. From the belay, traverse left with difficulty to gain the foot of a steep crack. It is wise to arrange protection here before moving on. Climb the crack to a resting place below a slabby groove. Pull into the groove, and climb this, exiting on the left into another groove which leads to a good ledge and belay. 4a) 30ft. Easy climbing leads to the top of High Man.

214 **Vandal** ** HVS
250ft. *G. Oliver, J. M. Cheesmond and L. Willis 1959*
A justifiably popular climb. Starts directly below the large triangular roof which is a prominent feature of the West Face.

1) 80ft. Scramble up the grassy corner to a stance 15ft. below the roof. Move right across the wall and climb up to a small ledge. Continue up a steep crack on the right with an awkward landing to a stance and belay. 2) 120ft. Climb the crack on the right to a small overhang at 40ft. From here make a long step left and climb the steep wall, or alternatively climb the overhang direct and continue up the corner, starting with a long reach. Either way leads to a fine slab which is climbed to a grass stance. Continue up for 20ft. to a belay below the final rib of Gomorrah. 3) 50ft. Climb the rib to the top of High Man.

89 *Pillar Rock, West Face of High Man, with Jordan Gap and Pisgah on the right*

215 **Rib and Slab Climb**   ***   S

300ft.   *C. F. Holland, H. M. Kelly and C. G. Crawford   1919*
Fine open climbing, on superb rock; one of the best slab
routes of its standard in the Lakes. Starts level with the
embedded block at the foot of the New West Climb and
about 40ft. to the left of it.

1) 60ft. The first 30ft. lead easily to a grass ledge on the left.
Step right onto a steep rib and climb this on good holds
until some small ledges on the left can be reached. A
reasonable belay on the upper ledge can best be utilised by
taking a stance on the lower ledge.   2) 25ft. The steep slab
above is bounded by a groove on the left. Climb the slab
with difficulty, or the slightly easier rib on the right, to a
ledge and belay.   3) 25ft. The groove above is gained by
an awkward move and leads to a stance and belay.
4) 40ft. Climb the steep rib on the left of the polished
groove of the New West to a stance and belay.   5) 70ft.
The route now takes the fine slab on the right. Traverse
right following a line of small incut holds until it is possible
to strike straight up the centre of the slab. At the top the
traverse line of the New West is gained, with a good block
belay on the right.   6) 80ft. Move up right for a few feet
then climb straight up the incredibly rough slab on the left
to reach the top of the crag.

216 **New West Climb**   ***   HD

290ft.   *G. D. and A. P. Abraham,
C. W. Barton and J. H. Wigner   1901*
An excellent route with varied climbing and good belays.
The rock is clean but very polished, so the climb becomes a
grade harder in poor conditions. Starts just below a large
block embedded in the scree a few yards to the left of the
deep gully (West Jordan Gully). The pitches described
below can be further split if desired.

1) 70ft. Slant left on easy rocks, followed by a rib to a small
corner. Continue up a steep staircase to a good ledge.

90 Opposite Looking down pitch 2, Vandal, Pillar Rock

*91 Overleaf left A typical situation on the West Face of High Man,
      Pillar Rock*

92 Overleaf right South-west Climb, Pillar Rock

241

2) 35ft. A wide chimney leads to a small platform, then a short traverse left is followed to a good belay.   3) 55ft. Climb an awkward groove, then a short slab and a delicate step left leads to the foot of a chimney.   4) 6oft. Climb the chimney with difficulty—a strenuous thrutch! The angle eases at 3oft., good belay but poor stance. From this point traverse horizontally right round the arete then ascend a pile of blocks to a large belay.   5) 4oft. Follow a difficult slab, trending right, to a corner and stance with belay 6ft. above.   6) 3oft. High Man is reached by a short chimney.

217 **South-west Climb**   ******   MVS
25oft.   *H. R. Pope and W. B. Brunskill   1911*
A superb slab climb with small but positive holds. Starts just left of the bottom of West Jordan Gully, the deep cleft separating the West Face of High Man from Pisgah, and takes the slabs which bound the right-hand edge of the face.
1) 3oft. Climb easy rocks to a grass ledge below a slab.
2) 85ft. Climb the slab, slanting up to the right, on small but good holds. A short steep section at 4oft. is overcome by a pull on excellent handholds, and leads to a small ledge and belay. It is usual to continue up the slab above for another 4oft. to another ledge and belay.   3) 75ft. Traverse left for 15ft. until it is possible to climb the slab up to the right on small holds. Traverse to the right towards the gully, passing under a large block, to a stance and belay.   4) 6oft. Return under the block and climb the steep rib to the summit of the Rock.

WINTER CLIMBING

Although Pillar Rock does face north, good snow and ice conditions are fairly rare. However, the gullies in the high corries beside the Rock regularly give pleasant Grade I–II snow climbs. In hard ice conditions, Walker's Gully can give a ferocious climb of Grade IV standard. Other climbs (such as the Old West Route and the other gullies) can give good climbs, but are very infrequently in condition.

LIST OF CLIMBS

WASDALE

Scafell Crag

Scafell East Buttress

Pike's Crag

Kern Knotts

ESKDALE AND DUDDON

248

BUTTERMERE AND NEWLANDS

Buckstone How

Eagle Crag

Grey Crag

Green Crag

High Crag

Dale Head Crag

Miners' Crag

ENNERDALE

Pillar Rock

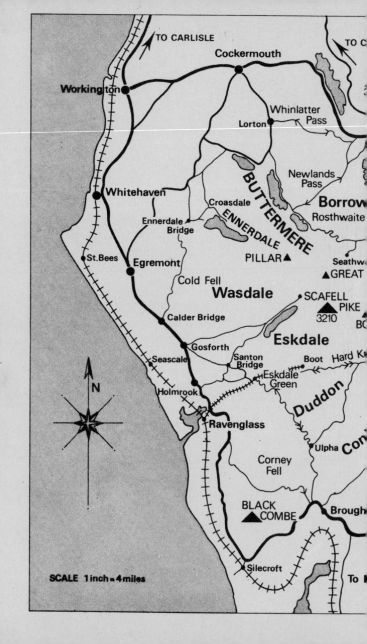